mjf

The Astrological Guide to Love & Romance

Sidney Omarr

MJF BOOKS
NEW YORK

Published by MJF Books
Fine Communications
322 Eighth Avenue
New York, NY 10001

The Astrological Guide to Love & Romance
LC Control Number 2001098733
ISBN 1-56731-487-2

Originally published as *Sydney Omarr's Astrological Guide to Love and Romance*, by Llewellyn Publications.

This edition published by arrangement with Llewellyn Publications.

Manufactured in the United States of America on acid-free paper ∞

MJF Books and the MJF colophon are trademarks of Fine Creative Media, Inc.

BG 10 9 8 7 6 5 4 3 2 1

Contents

The Astrological Guide to Love & Romance

Introduction

Astrology teaches us that almost every department of life is important and can be utilized to advantage—when understood.

I have been involved in astrology for all of my adult life: writing about it, debating the subject, using it as a tool for problem analysis. Perhaps I am the most published and publicized (through radio, television, and syndicated column) astrologer of our time. I do not claim to be the greatest because the more I learn the more I realize there is to know.

But I feel, because of my unique position, that I can tell what concerns most people most of the time. It is not sex. *It is love.*

It is love, financial security, and health—in that order: those are the concerns of more people more of the time than any other, based on the thousands of requests for guidance which I receive throughout the days, weeks, months, and years. *It is love* that is of the most concern, with money running as a Place bet, but far behind, while health, as a Show bet is safe, but very, very far back of love, which is by far the leader and the winner.

Where, then, is sex? It is there, in the Fifth House, that section of the horoscope which, among other things, is specifically related to sex. Love, on the other hand, permeates *all* of the Houses or sections of a horoscope.

Sex is but one factor of life and any attempt to make it more significant or to permit it to dominate is destructive rather than constructive. Sex is wonderful and healthy, but it is not love when taken alone. It is a part of love, but it is only in the Fifth House, one sector; it is not everything—and when famous or less known individuals consult me, it is not sex which is the predominant question: rather, the plaintive cry is for *love.*

Ideally, the combination should be *love and sex.* It is my intent here to guide you along lines which bring the two together, because that is as it should be. As it *should be,* not from any moral standpoint, because I am not a preacher; as a newsman, editor, and creator of documentaries, I have learned to be skeptical of "morality." I say *should be,* based on the discipline and experience one attains after years of utilizing the ancient scientific art of astrology to help people help themselves. If nothing else, astrology has taught me that, without love, there is very little else that is worthwhile. There can be an abundance of sex but it is mostly clamor and clang, sound and fury, when devoid of that mysterious ingredient symbolized by the word *love.*

This is not an attempt to downgrade sex. I love my two cats, but I would toss one or both out of the nearest window if one or both interfered with the kind of love that a man and woman have together when Mars and Venus are "at work," or when the Sun and Moon are "pulling" the emotional tides. Love without sex makes the world less likely to go around: Mars is positive (male) and Venus is receptive (female); the Sun is masculine and the Moon is feminine.

But it is love *and* sex together that are most important, and the two should go together, although they are, as I say, not necessarily one and the same.

To bring them together! Ah! There is the ideal: that's what I feel I can help you to do through these pages.

Latest research reveals or verifies that Scorpio people are the most passionate of lovers. Leo natives have been voted as "most skillful." Teachers given the responsibility of explaining sex to children in their classes bemoan: "We are trusted to teach the technicalities, from birth control to seduction. Nowhere in the curriculum is there a heading that reads 'Technique!'"

Adult men and women complain equally that too often the sex act is not performed as an artist would paint a picture—in other words, it is mechanical, with technique sadly lacking. I do not claim that in these pages I will make you a great lover, but you will be more aware, sensitive, creative, dynamic and will develop the kind of technique in making love that will cause you to be sought after by people who appreciate an artist at work.

Start with fundamentals. The Sun, giver of life, can be regarded as aggressive, the male. The Moon, passive, reflects the light of the Sun—the Sun takes initiative while the Moon is languidly, seductively receptive. Applying numbers, the Sun is number one, the Moon is two. Combined we have number three which relates to Jupiter, the lucky planet of joy. A union between the Sun (male) and the Moon (female) would ideally result in Jupiter, the astrological symbol of combined idealism, philosophy and sexual gratification.

About promiscuity: In astrology we learn that when one has an "affair" with another—that person's planets fall on the partner's horoscope and vice versa. Example: If you have a sexual relationship your partner's planets fall on your horoscope and planets and your planets fall on his or her horoscope as the case might be. The more "affairs" you have, the more of a jumble the horoscope becomes and your life will take on the aspects of an emotional jungle. An individual who brags about his or her "conquests" is admitting failure as a person and soon the life of the "conquerer" falls into the morass of a mess.

Doctor Sydney K. Bennett, Ph.D., a famous old-school astrologer, gave many examples of what happens to the honor, integrity, and self-esteem of those who make a steady practice of bed-hopping. If nothing else, astrology promotes a sense of discrimination and warns that "playing it loose" leads to "looseness" in all areas of life. Thus, the precious gift of sex, devoid of love, becomes tarnished and tattered.

In the following pages you learn how you relate to everyone else according to their zodiacal signs. You will, at the very least, elevate self-esteem. Ultimately this leads to "true love" and makes you a person who is not afraid to look into a mirror. When you do, you will be seeing yourself as a whole person and not as a frazzled, shattered human being. If only this is accomplished, this book will have served a noble purpose.

Aries

March 21 - April 19

You are quite sensitive to loneliness. Thus, once a contact is established, you tend to cling to it (you're similar in this manner to Cancer). The Fifth Sector of a chart is related to sex; Leo is your Solar Fifth House. The Sun of Leo combines with the Aries Mars to make you active where the love pattern is concerned. You can also be possessive, slightly selfish and domineering in this area. You are, moreover, exciting, magnetic, inviting and very attractive to the opposite sex.

I have noticed a psychological quirk about Aries in the sex area. You insist, for some reason, on attracting to you persons who use you and make demands, who really do not satisfy the empty well of loneliness.

Admittedly, some individuals are worth "hanging on to," but the odds are that you won't attract them until you learn when to let go of "the other kind." Admittedly, this is not easy. You confuse it with loyalty. You are determined that what you possess should be special, unique, of value. Thus, to let go is, in your mind, an admission that you made the wrong choice. But hanging on can deteriorate into a merry-go-round of contradictions and frustrations. There is nothing halfway with you—and this includes relations with the opposite sex.

Listen, Aries: I know how important it is for you to communicate your feelings. This need is actually a dilemma. And I'll tell you why. It is one of my revelations about you. You constantly worry because you feel persons who will understand, those to whom you can communicate, are a rare breed. You suffer silently, especially in the sex area. You won't open up. You won't say what is good, fair, wonderful or adverse for you. You won't say because you feel what you say will fall on deaf ears, or that persons will not comprehend, or will misunderstand or misinterpret.

Sex, for you, is a matter of impulse rather than deliberation. You are rash, impetuous, headstrong, impulsive where sex is concerned. In being so, you are on that constant journey, that search, seeking the ideal mate, partner. Where is the one, you ask, who will understand, comprehend, fulfill my needs?

Your doubt could cause you to choose and associate with "lesser" persons because that seems "safe." When you are the director, then (or so you think) you will not be vulnerable. Your emotions, you feel, will not be taxed. The relationship can be something of a lark. You are not exposed and, thus, you will not be hurt. Or so you think.

You are not challenged. *But neither are you happy with such a relationship.*

Your planetary symbol, Mars, is associated with action, aggressiveness. Combined with the Sun (your Fifth House ruler), this gives you a quality of regal beauty. You can, on the negative side, be haughty. But on a positive level, you can be warm to the degree of passion. You are creative, in sex as well as other areas. You find ways of expressing yourself which many might consider unorthodox. This applies to intimate as well as other forms of self-expression.

In your sex attitude, there can be a sense of abandon—or *resignation.* You give—often more than you receive.

The sign representing your Seventh House or marriage sector is Libra, associated with Venus. Thus, the three planetary symbols which are significant where sex is concerned are Mars (your ruling planet), the Sun (termed a planet, for the sake of convenience, and ruler of your Fifth or sex-activity sector) and Venus (ruling the sign of marriage in your Solar horoscope). This combination, Mars-Sun-Venus, makes you an idealist where sex enters the picture. There is fire and emotion—and the *excitement of discovery.*

There we have an astrological key: once a relationship becomes routine, you are disheartened. Once a relationship loses the element of romance, you lose interest. A famous actress, a leading lady born under Aries, once confided to me that romance was the very essence of her interest in sex. She required the *excitement of discovery.* She needed to be treated as a bride, one might say. Otherwise, she discarded her man and went in search of another who would perceive her needs, cater to her romantic whims.

Carried to extremes, this is a childish or immature characteristic. But, with sensitive balance (which Libra can often provide), this quality could add spice to any relationship and instill *life* into the everyday routine of living. Living could become loving—an experience, a happening rather than a mere occurrence.

Plainly, Aries, without love and romance, you have little interest in sex. Without these essential ingredients, you put us on. You pretend. You make concessions. And in so doing, you become irritated both with yourself and your partner.

For you, sex is not only romance, it is discovering that you can live as well as exist. It is something of which you want to be *proud.* Listen; you can be as cold as ice unless you have pride in your partner, loved one. But, once that pride exists, your fiery nature comes to the fore; you are warm enough for anyone, especially for yourself. Without pride, there is a letdown and sex becomes something you tolerate rather than enjoy.

You are warm, passionate and generous with your affections. Once you *accept* a person—you give. Once you have pride in an individual, you also *love.* For you, giving is linked with love, romance, and intimacy.

At times, you startle members of the opposite sex. You appear aloof on the surface, even haughty and disdainful. But once the surface is scratched, a new chapter has been written, a different story told. You give . . . and give; this, at times, causes others to "back off." They are startled, surprised. Some will become suspicious, seeking reasons and motives. Realize this and temper your display of emotions; take it easy lest your ardor cool your partner. By this, I do not mean to shut off affection; what is meant is that your love should unfold, rather than envelope completely, suffocatingly, suddenly, overwhelmingly.

It is not unlikely that you have acted impulsively in the love area—this has led to trouble, perhaps tragedy. You impulsively love the "wrong" person. You throw logic out of the window and permit emotions to rule. To find lasting satisfaction, it is necessary to exercise powers of discrimination. *Choose.* Be selective. You have too much to give—your "gifts" are too valuable to be wasted on an undeserving, immature, suspicious, grasping individual.

The physical side of relationships is extremely important to you. Without the feel, the touch, the embrace, there is an emptiness that is almost impossible to fill. Other zodiacal signs, of course, need physical love. But it is easier for others to adjust to deprivation than it is for you. To find fulfillment, to fill the void, you must find an individual who requires affection to a degree that some would consider "demanding."

In physical relationships, you are impetuous and passionate. But your *idealism* is ever-present. Once you mistrust or suspect, there is a coldness that settles over any relationship. Love doesn't last when this occurs; it freezes, is frigid.

When a relationship ends—when you are downcast, disillusioned—you tend to let down on principles and to accept partners beneath your socio-economic and intellectual level. Perhaps a psychologist would explain that this represents a method of self-punishment. As an astrologer, I would state that an Aries person, supersensitive about placing body and trust in what turned out to be the "wrong" hands, now seeks to prove that the body and trust must not have been worth very much.

In a sense, this is your way of fighting back, of stating, "I didn't really give or lose much because I didn't have much to give or lose, anyway." Aries, on the negative side, then engages in relationships with a number of persons—until emotionally exhausted. Then follows a "cool" period, after which—yet again—you seek one worthy of what can be given so fully, warmly, so passionately.

Listen: you are nobody's fool but you can do a good job of fooling yourself—especially in the love area. You want a relationship to be unique, special, separate from what others have had or experienced—so much that you could go overboard without a life jacket. Hold in reserve your dynamic qualities—until you are at least partially certain that you are giving to the right individual. If you are disappointed in others on numerous occasions, your guard goes up and is reflected in what appears to be sexual indifference. That need not occur if, in the beginning, you don't deceive yourself.

Children come to mean much to you; you regard sex as something which can and should lead to offspring. Children and sex are tied together in your makeup; sex, for you, can be serious and sacred. That's why, Aries, it is so important that you control your impetuous nature; control, discriminate and chose with care. Sex, for you, can lead to multi-faceted fulfillment: pleasure and children, home and creative living. Sex, for you, is no plaything. Don't fool yourself by entering into a relationship that you perceive will not be meaningful. If it is not to be significant, you will hurt yourself, perhaps despise yourself, punish yourself.

You desire to "show off" the object of your affection. To do so, respect and pride once more enter the picture: these are your "twins." Without them, you find it difficult to achieve real satisfaction. Perhaps, Aries, I am repeating myself in this area. But the points are important enough to bear repetition. Unless they are embedded in your subconscious, a substantial part of your life style will go down the drain.

Please don't expect your partner to be led, directed, instructed. You can create unhappiness if indeed this does become your expectation. Give and take on an equal basis—that should be your motto where affairs of the heart are concerned. Too often, where Aries is involved with the opposite sex, this is not the case. The fault, at those times, lies not with your partner, but with you. Regardless of whether you are a man or a woman, it is natural for you to take charge in any situation—but your partner has an equal stake and an equal say in the relationship, and your domineering traits could be most undesirable here.

Man or woman, you are attractive to the opposite sex. This, at times, causes you to indulge in flirtations. That's fine for fun and games—but I would not guarantee permanent happiness as a result of an overabundance in this kind of thing. It affects you in a negative manner; it causes you to regard yourself as cheap.

Another hint: the green-eyed monster is not apt to be a stranger to you. Learn how to cope with jealousy.

Have enough regard for yourself to push jealousy into the background. A certain amount can be flattering to your partner—an excess could lead to the kind of bickering which makes a honeymoon something that is a memory, finished.

Sex and you—not without complications, but an area of your life which could spell ultimate satisfaction and lasting happiness.

How You Relate to the Other Signs

Aries is harmonious in relation to Leo, Sagittarius, Aquarius and Gemini. Aries is not favorably aspected to Libra, Cancer or Capricorn. Aries can be considered neutral where the following signs are concerned: Taurus, Virgo, Scorpio and Pisces.

You are physically attracted to Leo persons. You harmonize with Aquarius and Gemini, and seem drawn to Sagittarians. There could be difficulties with Cancer and Capricorn, and the same applies to Libra, although there appears to be a legal tie involved in relations with natives of that sign.

Of course this represents the briefest view of how you relate to the other signs. There are further details, nuances, indications; let's elaborate on some of the highlights.

Aries with Aries

With another Aries, the relationship is one that is active, constantly striving, idealistic, concerned with universal appeal and faraway places. It could be quite fiery; both would want to assume leadership.

The Aries man is dynamic, wants you to dress with an air for the dramatic, abhors drab women—in or out of the sex area. The Aries man needs reassurance of your love—and he doesn't want routine hand-holding or caresses. He needs the warmth of passion. He comes alive if you take the initiative in demonstrating love. His sexual nature is one that could be described as fiery, intense.

The classic Aries man needs his ego—don't deprive him of it or you'll lose a quality which makes him very attractive, especially to you. All of us require our ego intact; but the Aries man, where sex is concerned, can be considered "a special case." His ego is his sex life. Leo requires ego in the love area, but it comes easy, naturally. For Aries, it is an essential, a hunger; without it, it is as if a man were on a hot, sunny desert and his water was taken away. That's what happens if you take away the Aries ego: he shrivels. The more this man thinks you appreciate him, the more he will respond, will return the compliment.

The Aries woman is not the kind you can lead in circles. She wants to know where she is going and has some ideas on how to get there. In loving her, don't fall into a routine or rut. Respond to her romantic flair. Lend fuel to her desire for experimentation.

This woman can be temperamental, headstrong, independent, and she can exude a kind of arrogance and sex appeal based on a blending of pride and willingness to give. Her standards are high; they are peculiar to her. Don't make her bend; she will be less of a partner, less of a person, less of a love if you try to break her. You will be unhappy because she will no longer be the vital, charming individual you were attracted to in the first place. You can't force her or push her, but neither should you fear the Aries woman. Nothing discourages her more than constant indulgence. She isn't easy to live with—but she is likely to be worth the trouble!

Being interested in an Aries man or woman is akin to taking a new lease on life. All Aries individuals have at least one basic characteristic in common: once they commit themselves, they give their all, they put their trust completely in the object of their affections. It is not difficult to see why, so often, they can be hurt, disillusioned and downhearted.

Aries with Taurus

Taurus persons are good for you financially. You also are physically attracted to the Taurean. Taurus is associated with Venus, while your ruling planet is Mars. These two planets, symbolically, represent physical attraction. The Sun of Taurus is in your Second House, which is associated with income, money, possessions, your ability to collect facts and figures, and to obtain legitimate bargains.

But, Aries, a word of caution. Taurus men and women may be a bit slow-moving for you. Aries tends to be aggressive, craves action, becomes impatient with one who procrastinates. Taurus is apt to ponder, analyze, make deductions—before taking any kind of action.

In a way, Taurus is good for you—he sets an example of patience. In dealing with Taurus for business purposes, you should not try to force your view or will. Taurus can be determined—and this determination, when carried to extremes, turns into downright stubbornness. If you've had any experience with the Taurean, you can verify this. In personal relations, the Taurus individual both *attracts* and *infuriates* you. You prod—you say, *Get going!* You say, I don't care what you do—but do *something.* And the more you prod, the more you push and cajole—the more the Taurus individual is likely to get his back up and to resist your efforts. Basically, the two signs are neutral in relation to each other . . . and Taurus is good for you where financial transactions are concerned. There's not as much fire, as in your relations with a Leo. But, then, Aries—perhaps you already have more than enough fire in your nature for one person.

You definitely are intrigued with Taurus; there is a sensuousness which emanates from these natives that "gets to you." In doing any purchasing, it is advantageous to have a Taurus with you. You could be lucky with bargains when accompanied by a native of this sign.

Aries with Gemini

The Gemini individual is restless, has numerous ideas and plenty of nervous energy. The Gemini Sun falls into your Third Solar House—and so you have very much in common. When you get together, there could be a gabfest to end all gabfests. In a sense, this is fine. But, carried to extremes, you both tend to scatter your forces. The key is to be selective, to choose the best. Gemini is Mercury and your significator is Mars. Gemini tends to give you a sense of direction, but also to tire you. This is because you find yourself moving, visiting, entertaining, being entertained. You tend to try to be every place at once when tied up with the typical Gemini native. Gemini makes you want to learn, to experiment, to report, whether that reporting be in the form of notes and eventually a story or article, or whether it succumbs to the temptation of mere gossip.

You won't get much rest being with a Gemini. But you won't be bored, either! The key is pacing. With a Gemini, your Third House is activated. This, to an astrologer, indicates that you have dealings with brothers and sisters, that you write, that you take short journeys, that you seek to improve your appearance because you get out and do things, because you meet people and because you are challenged by ideas. You come alive in a sense and your appearance becomes important. You *tingle.*

Gemini gets you going—sometimes. to the point of starting arguments. You can argue with Gemini, and Gemini can make you tired, but, Aries, you are also intellectually stimulated . . . and this is no small matter.

With Gemini, you can expect a plentiful supply of change, travel and variety. There is excitement generated and much activity. If your forces are properly channeled, this combination could be a profitable, satisfying one.

Aries with Cancer

Where the zodiacal sign Cancer is concerned, the aspect is not favorable, which means, Aries, that you have to work to make this relationship last. It doesn't happen by itself. You are a Fire Sign and Cancer is of the Water element. Persons born under Cancer activate your sense of responsibility. But on the negative side there is a tendency for you to feel tied down.

Cancer is good for you where your home and your property are concerned. Cancer also is favorable where long-range projects enter the picture. Cancer is associated with the Moon—and this brings together your Mars with the Moon, creating a male-female polarity and bringing about physical attraction.

Cancer's general effect on you is of a settling-down nature, of encouraging homemaking, of making you aware of what has to be saved for the proverbial rainy day. There are some blocks, oppositions to your relationship to the typical Cancer individual. But these are brought about, in the main, by a tendency for you to want to move, while Cancer wants to stay put. If you can reach an intelligent compromise, then all is harmony.

You can inspire Cancer and Cancer can calm you. Now, once this is balanced—the calmness and the inspiration—there is a fine relationship. Meeting and dealing with Cancer is part of your experience, for you tend to need a weight, a goal, an objective. The older Cancer individual may bear down a bit too hard, but you can ride with the storm. You're fiery and independent . . . and Cancer merely is attempting to channel your forces in constructive directions.

In enhancing security, the purchase of property, Cancer is good for you. But there is a tendency for resentment to build . . . for steam to be transformed from vapor into an explosive force: when this occurs the relationship could be over.

Aries with Leo

You get up and go with Leo; there is action and there are new starts in new directions. Your creative urge is stimulated; the Sun of Leo combines with your Mars to create physical response. Natives of Leo attract you in a basic sense; you are drawn, almost magnetized. The Sun and Mars combination symbolizes a spark, ignited into afire, which burns bright and quickly.

Leo affects that part of your Solar horoscope having to do with children, sex, creative endeavors, speculation. The two signs—Aries and Leo—are well aspected; the combination is excellent for enthusiasm, excitement, the creating of new methods, operations. With Leo, you tend to break off old relationships and to enter a new phrase of activity.

You may not feel secure, but you will feel alive. Energy burns in the manner of a Roman candle; with Leo, you are seldom in one place for very long. Questions are asked and answers demanded; intellectual curiosity bums brightly.

With Leo, there is much affection and some of it could be showered on children. The adventure of creating is evident; Leo natives inspire you to produce and to utilize basic abilities. An especially favorable relationship where new starts or projects enter the picture. If you want to break from the old, Leo is the individual to help you along pioneer paths.

You tend to regard Leo as your opportunity to express inventive qualities. If you want to play games with emotions, find someone else. With Leo, you could become inextricably involved.

Aries with Virgo

Virgo persons serve you, remind you, often bring about feelings of guilt. This is because Virgo represents your Sixth House, associated with basic duties, health, work.

Aries with Scorpio

Scorpio natives, in relation to you, represent intrigue. These persons often frighten you. This is because, Aries, they awaken your emotions—you tend to do and say things which you ordinarily would avoid.

The Pluto of Scorpio and your Mars represent rebellion; the status quo is overthrown. Your ideas are revolutionized. You engage in activities which you may previously have considered taboo.

Scorpio natives nudge your innermost desires. You may not immediately like Scorpio, but neither can you ignore Scorpio. Money, love, your well-being, your views—all are going to be challenged by your relationship to this individual.

The Scorpio relationship accents budget, the finances of your mate or partner, the hidden, the occult, the mysterious—and sex. Scorpio, at times, tends to smother you. Too much of one thing, too much at one sitting, *too much too soon.* That's how Scorpio could affect you.

You could feel restricted in association with Scorpio, because Scorpio reminds you of fiscal responsibilities. Scorpio makes you stop and dig and examine—and to a *varied* menu—then steer clear of Scorpio. But if psychological mystery intrigues you, you've found the right person.

Aries with Sagittarius

Sagittarius, in relation to Aries, is considered favorable. Both are Fire Signs, and here we have a combination of Jupiter for Sagittarius and Mars for Aries. Together, this produces expansion, much activity, a reaching out for more, a lack of satisfaction with the status quo.

For you, Aries, the Sagittarian seems connected with journeys and publishing, with education and knowledge. Sagittarius could be your teacher. You are encouraged by these people to experiment and to learn, to publish your findings, to develop the best you have, to adhere to principles and to let others know what you think and feel concerning major issues.

You seldom do things halfway when you are involved with a Sagittarian. For you, Aries, this association could result in long journeys, including *journeys of the mind.*

On the negative side, there could be plans too big to be practical. There could be delays. There could be such an air of optimism that practical issues are pushed aside.

Generally, Aries, this is a favorable sign for you—if you don't procrastinate, it could lead to a long-range project which pays handsome dividends.

As an experiment, Aries, check to see if your mate or business partner has any brothers and sisters who were born under the sign of Sagittarius. In a strictly classical astrological sense, this could be true. Get out your notebook; start checking dates!

Your sense of humor improves with Sagittarius. You enjoy travel in the company of Sagittarius. These natives help you expand horizons and are an excellent influence if you desire to write, advertise or publish.

Aries with Capricorn

With Capricorn, your sense of responsibility is activated. Capricorn could be good for your career. There could be some gloom here, too, because you work—and you learn lessons. Past efforts bear fruit.

Capricorn persons have the kind of effect on you which might be described as a *slowing-down process.* Capricorn is your natural Tenth House, associated with career, standing in the community, professional attainment. Where personal matters are concerned, Aries, you are fascinated by Capricorn. Often you look up to Capricorn as a father or mother image.

The Capricorn individual may help elevate you in a career or professional sense, may make you aware of duties, resolutions, responsibilities. *But unless you are mature you will rebel.* Don't feel or think you have found the perfect protector in the Capricorn. The Capricorn will soon do some rebelling of his own if you continue to lean, if you are arrogant, if you become over-dependent, if you expect too much, if you forget that friendship, or love, is a two-way street.

Unless you are grown up, unless the lines of experience are evident, it would be best for you to pass the Capricorn. But, in a professional sense, Capricorn makes a wonderful business manager for you. Capricorn can guide your career, can give you the benefit of experience.

The Saturn of Capricorn combines with your Mars to equal power, business acumen, executive direction. The relationship is not problem-free, but it is good for getting ahead.

Aries with Aquarius

Aquarius natives, in connection with you, emphasize the friendship angle of your chart—they activate the the hopes and wishes section of your Solar horoscope. Aquarius is not always good for you, even though it is favorably aspected to your sign. The Aquarian touches your aspirations, and when this happens, you sometimes wind up being let down. Sometimes you almost appear predisposed to be disappointed when it comes to living up to or fulfilling aspirations.

Aries, take special care when dealing with a member of the opposite sex born under Aquarius. These people attract you. They make promises. They are romantic. You want to believe and, in wanting to believe, you invite deception. This is a combination of Fire and Air . . . Aquarius being of the Air element. The heat grows in intensity as the flames are fanned by the Air. The Uranus of Aquarius combines with your Mars ruler to produce sudden action, quick responses, a vital friendship which could develop into something more serious.

However, there are blocks and restrictions. At times, the block is financial. Or it could be that you hope for more than the Aquarian can deliver. This can be a pleasant, fruitful relationship *if you are realistic.* Otherwise, you ask for trouble. You ride on a bubble which could burst in mid-air.

You are direct, frank, desiring to get directly to the heart of matters. But, in relation to an Aquarian, some of your strong points are weakened . . . you procrastinate, you make excuses, you cover up to save your pride.

For fun and games, this is a fine relationship; but realize that ultimately the game could become the real thing.

Aries with Pisces

With Pisces, you tend to brood, to have secret longings and fears. You want to give your best; very often you give more than you receive. You try, it would appear, to cleanse yourself of some real or imagined guilt. This seems to be the way Pisces acts on you. Pisces is a Water Sign; you are a Fire Sign. It is not easy for you to blend with Pisces. But, Aries, you certainly can *learn.*

Pisces stimulates you to study, to research, to appreciate privacy—and Pisces, in actuality, is good for your nerves, providing a sense of balance.

Basically, Pisces and Aries—together—make it difficult to arrive at facts. A kind of dreamy atmosphere is likely to prevail. The unexpected, the unseen, the hidden—these are emphasized for you when you connect with a Piscean.

Pisces is good for you on special study projects. But Pisces could also restrict you.

The Neptune of Pisces combines with your Mars significator to produce an air of mystery. With Pisces, there are apt to be clandestine meetings or activities. Pisces affects that part of your chart related to the hidden, to secret fears—and enables you to separate true friends from those who would merely "use" you.

You get the truth with Pisces—this is not always pleasant, but it is of value. You succeed with Pisces in charity drives, in financing a project sponsored by a special group, club, organization. However, Pisces and Aries—relating as individuals—are apt to lack staying power. The ties appear flimsy. To make this association succeed on the personal level, you are going to have to work at it. Neptune is illusion and Mars is action; the twain can meet if you're determined to pull the loose ends together.

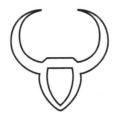

Taurus

April 20 - May 20

Your love pattern is strong; but sex and love are not necessarily the same. The two may require each other—but it would be a mistake to think they always go together. You attract unusual persons and situations in this area because you are seeking the out-of-the-ordinary. This is not to say you deliberately draw to you the bizarre, often the humorous. But it is to indicate that, because you are analytical, you quickly become bored with routine in love habits. The Fifth House is related to sex; Virgo is on the cusp of your Fifth Solar House. This brings Mercury into play here and causes you to be discriminating.

The fact, Taurus, is that those you attract *attempt* to whet your appetite, to heighten your interest. You often are *catered* to: where deep emotions are concerned you gravitate to those willing to serve, please, or enhance your pleasure. On the face of it, this cannot be considered negative. However, this does place pressure on your partner. It is somewhat like having to come up with a new act, a different story—and the danger is that something personal and sacred could become a performance rather than a spontaneous action.

The point, Taurus, is that you can chase love away by being too critical. You are sensuous. You have a great capacity for love. But in the sexual area you could be too demanding. Not that you are conscious of this; but your Venus ruler and the Mercury significator of your Fifth House' combine to indicate variety, excitement, analysis. That is the key word—*analysis.* You can become *too conscious* of what occurs during intimacy. It is a question of being able to abandon yourself to pleasure—which is not always easy for you in the sexual area.

You are, in this area, what some might term a *perfectionist,* others a *hedonist.* Frankly, Taurus, you are lusty in your approach to sex (depending, of course, on variations in your complete horoscope). Your appetites are strong, as reflected in your sexual drive. Often, however, you lose opportunity for fulfillment by assessing, evaluating, judging, comparing—and, at times, being jealous of your partner's past.

Your basic approach is healthy. You are not the kind of individual who substitutes pretty words for real meanings. You usually say what you mean—and mean what you say. Some regard this as offensive. Others recognize that sex is a part of life, not everything in life, but most certainly a major part of living.

Your love of comfort enables you to share with loved ones fine food, excellent living accommodations—and also highlights your very affectionate nature. Basically, you are faithful—until you feel you have been deceived, taken advantage of—then you seek retaliation, often in what might be considered a gross manner.

Like Cancer, you see sex as often linked with food. All the comforts of home—these are essential. And that, Taurus is why you don't usually wander, unless emotionally hurt. You simply are not the type to boast of conquests, to be promiscuous for the sake of promiscuity. Where Cancer keeps slim while in love—and gains weight when emotionally disturbed—you tend to put on weight when your love life is serene. When disturbed, you could lose interest in food. Cancer, however, could become a food glutton when "out of love." That's the difference in the two signs in this area. You respond well to Cancer. There is basic attraction. You are both practical about money—and love. But there lies the rub; you find Cancer too practical for your liking.

No one can force you into anything—but a wise member of the opposite sex can *lead* you with affection. That, Taurus, is what you need plenty of—affection. Oddly, perhaps, you associate affection with love more than you do sex. It would be wise to recognize that a *trinity* exists: affection, sex and love.

Some complain that you are not demonstrative. To a marked degree, this can be true. Some who are married to Taureans report to me that their Taurus mates very often indulge in periods of silence. Because these periods occur for no apparent reason, the Taurus partner can become confused, unsettled. Realize, this and consider the feelings of one close to you when you crawl into that emotional shell. Of course, for a restless, dynamic, high-strung person—such as Gemini—you could be a balm, a soothing tonic. As a matter of fact, you *are* intrigued by Gemini. You supply the stability and Gemini contributes ideas often profitable ones.

Basically, Taurus, you must be on guard against misplaced affection. Choose your mate with care—even if this means delay. Physical attraction is so important for you that, in the flush of excitement, you could overlook other important factors. For one example, you tend (on the negative side) to choose a partner who is critical of your habits to an extreme. Then, you could get the opposite—one who caters to such an extent that all challenge is gone, and, with it, excitement.

Whether you are a man or a woman, you are an individual who appraises, discriminates, is something of a *connoisseur.* This is applicable to sex as well as other areas. You want the best—but often accept less. Given affection and praise (somewhat like Leo), you will forego other, perhaps more practical assets. You are hungry for experience as well as food. Where love is concerned, you can be positively famished!

Vivian E. Robson, the late astrological sex authority, claimed that you have the power to *soothe.* In a way, this is true. You can assure others that all will be well—that a crisis will pass. This quality is important in love relationships. It relaxes.

Your sexual life is not without complexities. But this doesn't amount to anything that cannot be solved. Your greatest asset is *appreciation.* One outstanding defect is an obstinate insistence that your partner be molded to your way of doing things. While you want abandon in others, you are reluctant to lay aside your own inhibitions completely. You tend to feel that, because you are not likely to be fickle, others should ask for little or nothing more in the way of emotional security. You are good-natured while things go your way. But when they don't, you can show us a temper we never suspected you possessed.

Sex, for you, is tied up with friendliness—and fulfillment of hopes and desires. The key is to know just who is your friend, and otherwise. Your mental attitude toward your partner is of extreme importance. There is not likely to be real satisfaction while you bear a grudge.

More so than with the other zodiacal signs, a secure feeling in the financial area is important to you. Money worries could upset the apple cart of your sexual fulfillment. Some claim that you want too much, that your demands are too heavy. In actuality, however, you strive to give value for value received. This being so, you will go all out to provide happiness for one who pleases you.

It is not wise for you to marry for money. This builds resentment—and makes it almost impossible to give or receive satisfaction. This point is made here because you may be tempted; but, upon mature consideration, you should realize that this is not for you. You need to *share,* not to give or receive completely.

You are not able to tolerate a partner who displays an air of superiority. Some are intrigued by one who seems to know everything. Not you, however. Your emotions are basic; although you attract bizarre persons or situations, you prefer intimacy with one who is mostly conventional.

If you feel you are being "taken," you rebel. And when you do, it is akin to permitting a bull to run loose in a china shop. Broken dishes may be the least of the damage. Many might be surprised by the fact that sex, for you, may be more mental than physical. Anticipation plays a bigger role than perhaps you would care to admit.

Your feelings run deep. You need to be sure of your partner—so much so that, at times, you are accused of being possessive. This puzzles you. "What is mine is mine," is likely to be your response. You cannot fathom why your partner would want something other than what you desire. That's why, Taurus, I said you are basically conventional in outlook. You can be—and are—passionate, affectionate, warm, hungry for love; but *within confines.* You are not enamored with the idea of too much experimenting—*unless you so decide.*

It is not that you are slow. It is merely that you are not "fast." This applies especially during courtship. You don't want to be rushed, startled—especially not shocked. You want pleasure more than excitement. When the ship of security is rocked, you are desirous of "taking a powder." After intimacy, you tend to be overly analytical. This, carried to extremes, causes you to criticize the object of your affection. In a constructive manner, this is not objectionable. But, Taurus, you can go to extremes. When this occurs, it is conceivable that an affair of the heart could end.

To enjoy the fruit of love, you must be lenient. It is not mature of you to suppose that comfort and passion can be exchanged without a hair being disarranged. Perhaps our illustration appears ludicrous. But then, Taurus, you have a way of understanding major faults and of pouncing upon the innocuous.

Basically, the greatest block to your receipt of pleasure in this area is a pronounced tendency to be too analytical. To put it plainly—*your mind gets in the way.* You do too much questioning: why is this, is this right or wrong, am I going to be sorry, will the rent be paid, can we afford the new bedroom set, will we be on time for our dinner appointment, does he or she *really* understand—and so on and on. Sexual pleasure is, among other things, a sharing of pleasure and a display (in the deepest sense) of friendship. Those are the only real concerns; anything else, during a time of intimacy, could throw you off base and cause the sacrifice of genuine fulfillment.

Listen: you are excellent when it comes to giving advice to others in this area. Often, in fact, you find yourself in the role of counselor. But when it comes to yourself, much of your innate knowledge seems blurred. It is a matter of physician heal thyself.

Without sex, you are akin to an individual who is out in a hot desert without water. This being so, don't deceive yourself into believing that a good game of chess with one whose mind you respect can substitute for release of emotional steam.

You are not shy about speaking up when your partner displays a lack. This, basically, is healthy and constructive. However, you should not take offense when the situation is reversed. Don't be so fixed in habit patterns that you refuse to change. The key, obviously, is to be more flexible. Of course, these references are not confined to the physical act of sex. What is of importance is that you allow yourself to gain release without being so much concerned with the "why's" and the "what ifs." Learn to loosen your grip—on others and on yourself.

Once you stop confusing a tendency to be overly analytical with good taste, you will be on the road to healthy gratification. You will, Taurus, be taking a giant step toward happiness when you accomplish this minor (but monumental) feat.

How You Relate to the Other Signs

Taurus is harmonious in relation to Pisces, Cancer, Virgo and Capricorn. Virgo stimulates you sexually; Cancer appeals and titillates; Sagittarius unveils mysteries; Scorpio draws, intrigues, challenges and could represent a permanent relationship. Taurus is not favorably aspected to Leo or Aquarius. Taurus can be considered neutral in relation to Aries, Gemini, Libra and Sagittarius.

You are physically drawn to Virgo individuals; Pisces persons also attract you. Both Pisces and Virgo can give you pleasure, although, with Pisces, you are apt to get out more often, meet more people. Scorpio excites you, and challenges—Scorpio could be chased until *you* are caught. Aries persons intrigue you and there is definite physical attraction. You harmonize with Capricorn and share numerous characteristics. You tend to be earthy in your approach to sex and Capricorn responds.

Of course this represents the briefest view of how Taurus relates to the other zodiacal signs. There are further details, nuances, and indications. Let's take a look at some of the highlights.

Taurus with Aries

If you have to spend much time away from people, you would probably seek out Aries to share that seclusion. Aries touches that part of your Solar chart related to clubs, institutions, clandestine affairs, privacy and unique interests. The Mars of Aries is attractive to your Venus; there are many characteristics which are opposite each other. This sets up a magnetic pole; you are drawn to the Aries vitality. Aries is fascinated by your ability to ruminate, to finally arrive at a decision and head for a goal. Although you are zodiacal neighbors—next-door variety—you are poles apart as far as basic drives, motives and interests are concerned. This being so, you can learn from each other. On a deserted island, Aries would be the ideal companion for you.

Aries individuals tend to excite you in the manner that one is excited by a drama. Aries represents mystery for you. These persons attract you physically, but any relationship takes on a clandestine atmosphere. This means that, although you may feel drawn to Aries, it is in a subtle manner, not out in the open.

You succeed with Aries in theatrical or television enterprises. Aries can get you going, is good for you when it comes to organizing, to forming an association, a special interest group.

It is best for you to entertain Aries at home, with not too many others present. Otherwise, you tend to drift and Aries moves away from your sphere. If you go out for entertainment with Aries, your best bet is a motion picture. You can be alone in a crowd and enjoy it with Aries.

Taurus with Taurus

With another Taurus, there is a tendency to do much socializing but little work. This is because each is afraid of offending the other; there is instinctive knowledge that two persons determined to have their own way might not have any way. Thus, the fun and games are emphasized—but very little that is of practical value.

The Taurus man wants the best of everything but is not above complaining about the price. He is practical, earthy, has a healthy appetite—both in food and sex. He enjoys the basics: eating, sleeping, loving. You will have to keep an eye on his diet. He expects you to give completely of yourself—but is, at the same time, sensitive about your appearance. He is not above using coarse language, but is dismayed when an off-color word leaves your lips. He is not the easiest person to live with—but he is lusty, can be a good provider and can be relied upon during emergencies. He is anything but perfect, but he is apt to be all man. Give him loads of affection. Keep him well-fed and loved. In return, he can give you fulfillment and a great degree of emotional security.

To please the Taurus woman you must indulge her whims, but also know when and where to draw the line. This woman wants a man and if you are less than manly the relationship could go out the window. She, unlike some women, does not find weakness attractive in men. She likes comfort; she appreciates luxury. Give her what you can but insist that she live up to her end of any bargain. She is generally willing to give as well as to take; she can be voluptuous, enjoys good food and does respond in the sexual area. Be positive in expressing desires. She is capable of helping you fulfill them. She can entice, appeal, attract, mesmerize: she is seductive and lazy in a sexy manner. She can be stubborn but charming, and is capable of making you run a gamut of emotions. Win your way with her; don't try to force issues. She can be a wonderful ally, but a formidable foe.

Taurus with Gemini

Where Gemini is concerned, these people activate your Second or money House. Gemini natives interest you because you can talk to them about your ambitions, your collections, your desires—but somehow it is difficult for you to really get excited about them.

With Gemini, there is much talk. There is planning and sharing of knowledge, ideas. Some of those ideas could click. And that's where the financial angle comes in. Gemini can be instrumental where money is concerned. But you could also get bogged down in a fog of plans, talk, and speculation. You could go too far out if you fall too much under the influence of charming Gemini.

Your Venus significator combines with Gemini's Mercury to bring about a kind of active receptivity. That is, Gemini does the talking and you do the listening. Gemini gives and you receive. This goes on until a balance is achieved . . . until you start giving. But, if you refuse to tackle your fair share, then there is a break-up—it is the end of Gemini and Taurus.

Basically, this kind of association can be amusing—and can fatten your bank account. But Gemini takes only so much—and soon you will be doing the *paying* as well as the collecting. Gemini is apt to lose patience with you unless you continually show interest, even awe, when Gemini speaks. If you're an energetic Taurean, then the association proves beneficial. Otherwise, Taurus, look elsewhere!

Taurus and Gemini often arrive at the right money decisions—they can be at the right place at the right time. There could be a "Midas touch" here, but once a point is proven the lines holding you together might snap. Gemini is active while you are apt to be passive where this relationship is concerned.

Taurus with Cancer

Where Cancer is concerned, you are stimulated mentally, but also you are apt to feel restricted. You want to break loose. You want to break shackles, imagined or otherwise. This is a case of the Cancer Moon and your Venus; you could make beautiful music. But there is apt to be a lack of solid foundation. Where a relationship here enters the picture, there is apt to be travel for you. Cancer stimulates your Third Solar House, which relates to your relatives, to short trips, to get-togethers, to ideas, mental pursuits.

But there could also be some sharp disagreements. Cancer may attempt to discipline you in a manner which causes lack of freedom, and here you can be stubborn.

Cancer, thinking of the future and of security, puts his foot down. Then the honeymoon is over!

Now, listen, Taurus: you can have a beautiful relationship with the Cancer native. But you may have to give a little, may have to let loose, may have to express yourself to a greater extent than usual. This doesn't make you feel comfortable. Both Taurus and Cancer have much in common: the same attributes, the same faults, the same assets, the same deficits. When Cancer and Taurus are put together, the result is responsibility. Which means, Taurus, this is no time to play games.

If you want to experiment, if you want to have a superficial relationship, look elsewhere. Cancer plays for keeps where you're concerned. So, Taurus, if it's fun and games you're seeking, cross Cancer off the list.

For permanency, security, a sharing of interests and ideas, Cancer could be ideal. It is a matter of your level of maturity.

Taurus with Leo

In association with Leo, you react in a manner which affects later years of your life, your security, home, and chance to gain a financial foothold.

The Leo individual causes you to fill in the gaps, to be aware of weak spots. Leo tends to give you a sense of what you need or lack. With Leo, you tend to be uncertain. You want to erase this uncertainty. You want to know where you stand. Leo makes you aware of what can be done—and, on the positive side, Leo makes you do something about it. On the negative side, you merely express doubt, become discouraged and finally brood.

Listen, Taurus: Leo is a good experience for you. But you may not be able to take too much of Leo at one sitting. It is like rich food. Fine for a dessert, or a change—Leo is a luxury. But eventually, the practical side of your Taurus nature comes soaring to the forefront. You begin to doubt, to check, to try to see persons or situations in a realistic light.

Leo is flashy where you are concerned. You smile outwardly, appear entertained outwardly. But, Taurus, inwardly you are apt to cringe because Leo is extravagant in your eyes. You then begin to check your own holdings. You check your assets and your debts.

Leo makes you aware of home, authority, what you owe and what you have coming to you. Leo is not favorably aspected to Taurus—but you can stand a little Leo in your life.

The Sun of Leo and your Venus ruler make an attractive combination: but, in the main, it is romantic rather than solid. Leo shakes you up, but the two signs are not well aspected. Good in some areas, but both can be stubborn and Leo will insist on the spotlight.

Taurus with Virgo

Virgo affects the section of your chart related to love, change, creative endeavors, adventure and speculation. Virgo encourages you to follow through on a hunch, to gamble on your abilities, to invest in your ideas, talents.

Virgo persons attract you physically—and you have much to learn from persons born under that zodiacal sign. The very best qualities of Virgo draw you, make you want to give of yourself. The less admirable qualities, such as a tendency to be overly critical, give you a view of when you're tearing down that which means the most to you.

Virgo, like Gemini, tends to stimulate you. These people sharpen your intellectual curiosity. Virgo, generally, is favorable for you—touching that part of your chart associated with children, creative activity, self-expression.

Once inspired by Virgo, you really get going and it is hard to stop you. You do benefit from such a relationship. It teaches you much about yourself, enables you to bring forth creative resources—and certainly you are attracted in a physical sense. This could be a fine thing, if you achieve a balance between the intellect and emotions.

Your Venus and the Virgo Mercury activate interests in art and creative subjects. Your intuition is sharpened by this relationship. You are not apt to be satisfied with the status quo; you want change, travel and variety. This is unusual for you, but that's the effect Virgo is likely to produce.

Taurus with Libra

Libra persons serve you well, but tend to give you a guilty conscience. This, Taurus, is because the Libra person has a way of waking you up, making you realize the vast extent of your potential. You begin asking yourself if you're doing enough. When the answer is negative, you fret, worry, castigate yourself.

Libra is associated with Venus, just as is your sign. When the two of you get together, there is apt to be a fine social time—and a scattering of forces. This leads you to an awareness of work neglected. It makes you feel guilty. You are attracted to Libra, but there is not too much that is accomplished. You tend, when with Libra, to find excuses for putting off today what can be done tomorrow.

The relationship could be described as ultra-rich, perhaps too rich. It could be too much of a good thing. Libra tends to want to serve you, to do you favors—and the more Libra does for you, the more you tend to resent it. It could be a complicated situation.

Listen, Taurus: if you want to gain constructively from such a relationship, try to achieve balance. Libra certainly will appreciate that—and you will gain in the long run. So, Taurus, if you find yourself leaning back, being waited on . . . change the rhythm. Start helping yourself, start returning the favor. That's how to make the most of your association with Libra.

Libra can make you aware of health, can aid you in elevating job opportunities, can enhance your appreciation of arts and crafts. Libra gentility has a tendency to rub off. You can gain through the association, especially if willing to listen and observe.

Taurus with Scorpio

You are attracted to Scorpio persons much in the manner that opposites attract opposites. The relationship, (although often resulting in marriage or other legal contracts), is usually either very good or very bad, with little in-between.

There is action when you get together with Scorpio. You tend to begin new projects, Taurus, in association with Scorpio, that could result in a business, a marriage, a contract, an agreement. There is a natural attraction, but both Scorpio and Taurus want to be the boss. This, of course, could lead to trouble—so, at the very beginning, it is best to settle just *who* is to take the lead.

If you want to pioneer, to begin a project, then Scorpio is perfect for you. But such a relationship does not promise to be completely smooth. Scorpio affects your Seventh Solar House, connected with marriage, contracts, the way you look to others. Scorpio can make you change your ways—and your appearance. Know this, be ready to make adjustments. This is a combination of your Venus and Scorpio's Pluto. Venus and Pluto can create new fashions, styles and can attract wide attention.

This is a relationship that could result in marriage. It also could finally be one in which both Scorpio and Taurus feel that it is time to move on, without the other. It is a relationship of extremes: either hot or cold, together for always, or a final parting. The accent is on publicity, contracts, and legal maneuvers. The key for both Scorpio and Taurus, in this relationship, is to learn temper control. If this is done, the relationship could survive a rocky beginning and go on to a glorious finale.

If it's peace and quiet you're looking for, then it is best to bypass Scorpio. But if you seek adventure—and are willing to make some very real changes—you have found the right person.

Taurus with Sagittarius

Sagittarius individuals represent the allies gained when you least expect them. Sagittarius possesses a unique kind of attraction for you—sexually and financially. Which means you are puzzled, fascinated, awed—almost all at once.

You have difficulty getting to the bottom of the Sagittarius personality. You are puzzled, at times mystified. This is the Jupiter of Sagittarius and the Venus of Taurus, with Sagittarius activating your Eighth House. This means, Taurus, that you go far afield. You attract questions, problems. You carry added responsibility. It is not an easy relationship, but could prove worthwhile. You enlarge horizons, you reach out, gain new interests—and also attract new problems. Sagittarius does provide challenge—and, Taurus, you require challenge in order to live up to the best in yourself.

You can build for the future with Sagittarius. But some of your objectives require review. There is a tendency, with Sagittarius, to take an unusual turn in the road. Caution is required. Patience becomes a great virtue here.

In relationship with Sagittarius, you must clearly outline objectives . . . and must finish what you start.

Sagittarius is a test and a challenge for you. If you are ready to put forth best efforts, then, Taurus, you can succeed in this association.

Together, Taurus and Sagittarius attract others—along with their problems. The two could make a good counseling team. Sagittarius activates your relations with those putting money trust in your hands. It is a very good idea, with Sagittarius, to inaugurate an investment counseling service. Sagittarius inspires you to reach beyond current concepts. Your ambitions are stirred; your reticence is shaken. The combination of Venus (Taurus) and Jupiter (Sagittarius) is pleasant, and could result in beauty and profit.

Taurus with Capricorn

Where Capricorn is concerned, these people are good for you—they inspire you to greater heights, but you often think of them as teachers or grim task masters. You don't have an easy time of it with Capricorn, because this sign represents your Ninth House—meaning higher education, long journeys, aspirations, philosophy, philanthropic enterprises. This is good, especially where publishing and writing are concerned. Capricorn also is favorable in connection with preparing an advertising campaign. No, not easy, but you are *inspired.*

There is certain to be physical attraction here—both Capricorn and Taurus are Earth signs—and Capricorn's Saturn lends reality, a solid base to the Taurus Venus, which can be flighty.

You can succeed in a relationship with Capricorn. But first, an understanding must be reached on an *intellectual* level. There must be mutual respect. You can't dive headlong into this association. Capricorn expects much of you. And until you are mentally conditioned to read, write, to expand and broaden your horizons, such a relationship would be premature and almost destined to break up.

If, however, you are prepared to grow, to break down barriers, and to enlarge your scope—this indeed can be a very fulfilling association.

Capricorn subdues your tendency to act on impulse. You are encouraged to view questions with the idea of obtaining answers. This means you think before you act. Saturn sobers you so that you become more analytical.

Your appetite for travel is sharpened—and, in a literal sense, Capricorn whets your appetite for foreign foods.

Your horizons will broaden—and if you are ready, latch on to Capricorn!

Taurus with Aquarius

In connection with Aquarius, these persons could have much to do with your career. The Aquarius individual touches that part of you connected with ambitions, aspirations . . . and the relationship between Taurus and Aquarius can be a harmonious one.

Aquarius, like your own sign, is fixed. Both of you are stubborn, tend to be set in your ways—you are both determined and you both want to lead the way. Aquarius is Uranus and, combined with your Venus, this could lead to bizarre situations. You have loads of fun with Aquarius. You encounter new experiences. If you want any rest, you won't stick to Aquarius. But, if you want excitement, intellectual and otherwise, you have found your match!

The Aquarian touches that part of your chart which affects your position in life . . . your goals, ambitions, profession, your business, your standing in the community. But, where Aquarius is concerned, you want to be the boss. And where you are concerned, the Aquarian is apt to think he, or she, knows what is best. It is likely to be a case of too many generals and not enough soldiers.

Two fixed signs, such as Taurus and Aquarius, could lead to a stalemate. If you are ready to make intelligent concessions or are willing to listen to reason to present your arguments in a logical manner, then you and Aquarius could have a chance together.

Uranus (Aquarius) and Venus (Taurus) blend to create emotional ups and downs. The relationship is not problem-free; it is one which requires discipline if it is to succeed. However, where business projects are concerned, Aquarius helps you fulfill aspirations and ambitions. Aquarius can lead you along new, adventurous paths—but you may not be a willing follower. And that, Taurus, is the crux of the matter.

Taurus with Pisces

Pisces people help you achieve your hopes and wishes—and you number many of them among your friends. Pisces affects that part of your Solar horoscope associated with friends, hopes, and wishes. Your fantasies also are activated through your association with the Piscean. It is a case of the Pisces Neptune, combined with your Venus, which can be beautiful, but impractical. It can be illusion which never turns to reality. But, on the positive side, you also *can* turn dream into actualities. You can transform ideas into solid projects.

Listen, Taurus: Pisces is favorable for you. But you might expect too much. You could be setting Pisces on a pedestal. You could waste time, money and emotions. You must bring forth your Taurus practicality. Otherwise, you find yourself living in a dream world with Pisces. You spend and travel; you are extravagant, you wish and dream—and you never quite get down to business. There is definite attraction here. But what is needed is a solid approach, an *understanding.*

If you are serious with a Piscean, you'll need to come to an understanding of what it is you are to accomplish.

Then adhere to resolutions. Otherwise, Taurus, you find that you have been living a fantasy. Much pleasure is indicated, but you tend to skip essentials. If you can draw the line between wishing and direct action, then this can be a wonderful association. Otherwise, with Taurus, you have fun, but lack funds.

Know this—be prepared for it—take steps which will make the most of what could be a very fine relationship. Pisces will encourage you, give you confidence, lead you to new social directions, get you out of the house, introduce you to stimulating people. But your *cooperation* is an essential ingredient. Without it, it is "no go."

Gemini

May 21 - June 20

For you, love is equated with balance, justice, equality, a sharing of joys and tribulations: you cannot have a fulfilling relationship with a partner who dominates, who takes without giving, or who lacks sensitivity.

The Fifth House of a horoscope is related to sex, among other things. Libra is on the cusp of that sector of your Solar chart. Venus rules Libra, and combines with your Mercury ruler in a favorable manner. But, for you, sex is favorable only when a large degree of genuine affection is present. When it is not, much brooding occurs; your emotions are shaken and the experience generally lacks satisfaction. This applies for both male and female natives of Gemini.

For you, sex is creativity—it is a rising above the petty; it is a giving of yourself in a grand manner. You give in order to receive. But, if it is one-sided, with your partner doing all of the taking, then the sex experience gives pain rather than gratification.

Your curiosity, however, could get the better of you. Because you become "involved" with people, one step could follow the other. Thus, you find it not impossible to love more than one person at a time. This is especially applicable during youth. But you do learn from experience. And experience will verify that you can only be happy in this area when you settle your affections.

Promiscuity is your barrier to contentment; happiness cannot be found by you during any phase of experimentation. It is fine to be curious, bright, charming: but sexual conquests do *not* represent a key to your happiness. For you, sexual gratification goes hand in hand with mental satisfaction. This adds up to respect—for your partner, for yourself. If that ingredient is lacking, fulfillment will also be absent.

You often make it difficult for yourself to gain satisfaction in this area. You want love, tenderness. But your Mercury ruling planet makes you an *analyst.* To find love, the subconscious must come through; the conscious or censoring mind, to a great extent, must be put to rest. You must let your guard down without overexposing yourself.

This may be difficult to comprehend. But it is as basic as saying "let nature take its course." That is, *after* you have been selective, *after* you have achieved mental compatibility, *after* you are confident of justice, of a fair deal . . . *after* that, stop analyzing!

Sex, for you, is largely on a mental level. You are apt to be a bundle of nerves, of energy; you are restless, seeking, probing, curious. Yet, it is important for you to relax in order to enjoy sex. That's why, Gemini, it is such a great matter when you do find the right person. When you do you can relax, you can lower your guard without fear that you are going to be used or hurt.

Emotional turmoil leaves you hanging on the ropes. Thus, you fear it and you are on guard against it. This does not make it easy for you to find fulfillment, in comparison to many of the other signs, to many other persons. But it is possible, even *likely.*

You are a giving person; you are basically warm, affectionate. But you have apprehensions about being restricted, tied down, having your emotions imprisoned. You could associate sex with a kind of discipline which will engulf your personality, making self-expression difficult. These are some of the mental acrobatics which can stand in the way of fulfillment.

One authority claims you are cold-blooded in the sexual area. I think not. It is merely that you are addicted to psychological analysis; you want reasons, you want to know the why of almost everything. You want to bring others out of themselves. In so doing, you may appear cool and aloof. In reality, you *are seeking to extricate yourself.*

Obviously, you are not the most uncomplicated person where sex is concerned!

You constantly seek an ideal. Once you do unlock the "mystery" of another individual, your own interest could wander. This leaves others puzzled, wounded, wondering what went wrong. On the positive side, knowing someone could be loving someone. That depends on your degree of maturity. Familiarity should *not* breed contempt.

The problem, Gemini, is that it is *you* who fears that being known, understood, or analyzed will cause others to lose interest. Once this fallacious attitude is comprehended and overcome, you stand a greater chance for security and happiness. It isn't necessarily easy, but it is *necessary*. Realize your own worth. It will be then—and only then—that others will appear worthy. Analyze that, Gemini!

Listen: you have a marked tendency to build people to gigantic proportions. When an individual fails to take giant strides, you are disappointed. You read meanings into statements; you depict moods. Often what you "read" or think you detect is simply a product of your imagination. The key is to accept an individual for what he, or she, actually is—not to imagine a person to be something entirely different. Until you learn to cope with the real person, you will be shutting yourself off from satisfaction.

You tend to be quick, impatient, irritable if others are slow to perceive, understand or react. On the positive side, you are challenging—causing others to keep up, to bring out the best in themselves. For success in sex, Venus must calm down your Mercury. Which, perhaps, is another way of stating that you can achieve a greater degree of happiness once you learn that sharing is what counts—not mere giving or taking. To share in a true sense, you must mature. That is not always easy when you are concerned. You are on the move, striving to improve, to refine, to pick up loose ends and fit them together.

For you, sex equals beauty, justice, the scales of balance—this, as stated, is an ideal state for you. Finding it is another story, because you stand in your own way. Once you obtain a desired object or goal—or person—you experiment. Should this be all I receive for *me?* That is apt to be one of your questions to yourself—and to your many confidants. Gemini, you do talk too much about intimate matters—often, to the wrong persons. The advice you receive is based not always on knowledge or wisdom, but on guesswork, on speculation, on a need for the other person to feel important. You give too much of yourself away through mere talk, gossip, questions.

That's the way it is with you, Gemini. You are on the go; some find it almost impossible to maintain the pace. However, where love is concerned, you would prefer to settle down, to relax, to revel in affection. Then, one might well ask, what is it that finds you involved with more than one person: why is it that you often marry more than once?

The answer, Gemini, must ultimately come from within. On the surface, you claim interest flew away, that a relationship became intolerably dull. Beneath the surface, the answer is apt to be something quite different. Your thirst for experience needs quenching. It isn't that you want to hurt or mislead others; it is that you want to taste and test, to travel and be aware, to analyze, question and find answers. With it all, you see (in sex) the kind of balance that will bring you peace.

Things that go bump in the night intrigue. The unknown is where you want to tread. But all of the time you seek the "known," the virtues that will bring security, love, affection, satisfaction. You are at odds with yourself in this area. Those who offer the greatest hope of understanding of the perplexing "you" are apt to be born under Aquarius, Libra and your own sign, Gemini.

Boiled down, it all comes to this: respect yourself first and become satisfied with what you have to offer; then you'll attract someone who, in turn, actually lives up to your ideals.

Sex, for you, is an ideal. It is not a mere act. It is not a technique. It is an all-engulfing experience. It can bring peace and contentment, as well as excitement. It is important for you. Without sex in its creative, mature, fulfilling sense, you are that twin, ever wandering, searching.

The search is for the other half of yourself, for that elusive quality—wholeness. Certainly, you are Gemini the *Twins.* But what you seek is to pull yourself together to oneness. This is especially applicable to sex. You equate sex with love, despite appearances to the contrary. You are intuitive about sex. You are subjective, although you think of yourself as analytical. If the truth be known, one part of you is the constant analyzer, in other areas as well as sex. Basically, however, it is a subjective, romantic feeling which draws you in this specific area. It is when that half of the twin becomes the analyst that you invite difficulty.

Many consider you fickle. These persons are viewing the curious analyst part of you. Those who understand the "other half' know that you can be constant—that your curiosity is a part of you, not the whole.

You are mentally quick; you make a good student, and are possibly an innovator. But in all your searching, you are on the path of security. To satisfy basic urges, you seek an ideal. Often, the *ideal* becomes mixed up with *idol.* Then the idol crumbles, has feet of clay. That's the key, Gemini: to pursue an ideal rather than an idol. If you differentiate, you are wise. If not, you are foolish.

A sex symbol born under your sign was the late Marilyn Monroe. She, too, was a searcher who very often confused *ideal* with *idol.* It is not an idol you need—*you should be your own idol.* And if you live up to the best in yourself, you will attract what you need in this, the vital sex area.

One of your characteristics is dedication. You become dedicated to a subject, an individual—then, quite often, that dedication shifts, the sands run and the search begins yet again.

Simply put, you must learn to dedicate yourself in a manner that brings benefits, not nervous exhaustion. You are not going to find fulfillment by willing it. You are going to find it by letting it happen. Life, for you, can be a glorious happening—if you permit it to be.

Don't rush. Be active, aware, *alive,* without feeling you must mold and guide. Offer guidance but don't force it. Be a teacher, not a director. Permit the Venusian side of your love nature to shine. What a difference it will make!

Your mercurial side can cause utter confusion in the sexual area. It is when you *think* too much that joy is held back, that the creative forces are blocked. Permit nature to have its say; give that motor-like mind of yours a rest!

Sense of humor—yes. Overanalysis—no. Balance—yes. Pinpoint accuracy—no. Ideal—yes. Idol—no.

In this simple yes-and-no technique lies the answer to contentment for you. You can understand this; it appeals to your desire for mental exercise. This lesson can make a vast difference in your outlook, your life. All else being equal (assuming you are with a person whose horoscope blends with your own), you can now put an end to the wandering, can come home to sexual fulfillment.

That, Gemini, is accomplishing a lot—especially while off the psychiatrist's couch!

How You Relate to the Other Signs

Gemini is harmonious in relation to Aries, Leo, Libra and Aquarius. Gemini is not favorably aspected to Virgo or Pisces—the sign is in opposition to Sagittarius and generally neutral to Taurus, Cancer, Scorpio and Capricorn.

Libra and Aries individuals attract you in this area, with emphasis on Libra. Capricorn, too, could play a major role here. However, it is likely to be Capricorn who frightens you. It is not easy for you to be free and easy with Capricorn. The Saturn of Capricorn restricts. You fear you may be confined. With Libra, however, you play the role of reformer. Aries argues. Aries could fatigue you. But, nevertheless, Aries is paramount in this area. What starts out as a friendly dispute could flare; the heat of conflict could be transformed into sexual response.

Of course this represents the briefest view of how Gemini relates to the other zodiacal signs. There are further details, nuances, indications. Let's elaborate on some of the highlights.

Gemini with Aries

Aries individuals affect that section of the Gemini chart related to hopes, wishes, friendships. You are attracted to

Aries. The attraction can grow into love. Listen, Gemini: you might start out playing games with the Fire Sign, Aries. But don't play with fire if you are not prepared to get burned. The relationship here can be favorable . . . if you are prepared for the consequences. Those consequences include a lasting relationship, physical attraction, a linking of hopes and desires.

Many of your friends are Aries natives. Together, Aries and Gemini create adventure, travel opportunities. Your creative urges are accented. You love change, adventure, travel. With Aries you could find the perfect companion or mate. But you both tend to tire each other. Realize, Gemini, that Aries does like to lead the way. And you have some ideas of your own—you tend to be experimental and you don't take kindly to regimentation.

You have a lot to learn from Aries. But, in the process, you could be rubbed the wrong way. Expect a fascinating relationship . . . but the road is not smooth. You will have to arrive at an understanding. Otherwise, much of your energy will be spent in arguing, in conflict.

Generally, Aries *is* favorable for you. Your interests are heightened. You read. You write. You express opinions. You travel. Very exciting—if you first decide that Aries is going to be the boss, no matter what!

The Mars of Aries and your Mercury ruler blend to produce excitement, travel, a tendency to argue . . . but a basic attraction which makes it a pleasure to reconcile. Aries may force you to get down to business where ideas are concerned. If you don't mind being led, eventually Aries could be instrumental in aiding you toward goals, toward fulfillment of desires.

Gemini with Taurus

Taurus individuals make you aware of your fear. Taurus tantalizes because you find it difficult to understand the true Taurean. Listen, Gemini: you can make this a successful relationship if you rise above petty complaints. Taurus inspires you to see a project as a whole, not in bits and pieces. If willing to share knowledge, to learn and to teach, then this becomes a profitable association.

Taurus persons affect that part of your chart related to the unseen, the unexpected, the hidden—the mysteries of life. Taurus also encourages you to join organizations, clubs, groups. Taurus encourages you to enter institutions of higher learning.

You are attracted, yet also have apprehensions concerning the Taurus person. Taurus shakes the skeletons in your closet. Secrets are revealed—you learn to live with the true facts of your life. Taurus stands fast and encourages you to unburden yourself of problems. Gemini and Taurus are neighbors of the zodiac, side by side. But both signs exhibit almost opposite qualities. Perhaps, Gemini, that's why you are fascinated by Taurus.

While you are restless, Taurus is fixed in nature. While you are on the move, Taurus very often is stubborn and adverse to change.

There is a tendency for you to become bogged down in this relationship. Unless you are willing to make some major concessions, such an association does represent problems. But you are no stranger to trouble, Gemini. And Taurus could help settle you, could bring a needed element of stability to your life.

The Venus of Taurus blends with your Mercury ruler to highlight intuitive qualities. With Taurus, there are clandestine meetings; secrets are shared. A romantic atmosphere prevails. But the relationship could lack balance, leaning one way or the other. Your restlessness and the Taurus tendency to stay put could create problems.

Gemini with Gemini

With another Gemini, there is action. You begin projects. You renovate and revise; you modernize. The relationship is stimulating. Ideas are transformed into action. With another Gemini, there are inventions, pioneering projects. Impulse rules and the pace is quick.

Gemini women are most appreciative of gifts and surprises. Flowers, followed by a theater party, will help her to realize your worth. Always remember, she doesn't want to be tied down or restricted.

Gemini women can also exhibit a disturbing habit: they laugh at the wrong times. A romantic moment—you wish to say or do something momentous—and Gemini is laughing. Laugh with her! Here's a warning: when you get used to them, Gemini women can become indispensable. But if you let them know it, you could be in for trouble!

Loosen the reins: the less you appear dependent, the more you will be depended upon. She has a great sense of humor—for this, you can forgive much. It is a great and wonderful quality. With her, you can be exasperated: your nerves will tingle, sometimes with joy—at other times, simply because you're becoming an emotional and physical wreck! But listen: she can be worth it!

The Gemini man barks loud, but his bite is a mere nibble when it comes to chasing other women. Remember this: don't try to inhibit him through jealousy. If you do, he. is apt to rebel—then the bite equals the bark. You can lose him through possessiveness. Give him plenty of room and he'll come home—to make a home, to make you happy.

He is versatile, alert, charming and blessed with loads of energy. No matter what the weather, he is willing to go out, to be on the move, to experiment, to satisfy his curiosity. He may tire you, but complaining has an adverse effect. He may agree you have a right, at times, to be downcast. But, in reality, he expects you to keep your chin up, to keep smiling and to be disgustingly healthy! With it all, he can be more than satisfactory. Hold on to him—but be subtle about it!

Astrological authority Vivian E. Robson has declared the following: "The wife or husband of a Gemini native must never be mentally dull or obtuse if happiness is to be maintained."

Gemini with Cancer

Cancer activates that part of your Solar horoscope associated with money and personal possessions. Your Mercury, combined with the Cancer Moon ruler, produces a tendency toward moodiness. Ups and downs in the emotional area are not uncommon in this relationship. An element of self-deception exists. You tend to view Cancer in an idealistic light. When flaws appear, you are surprised. If, however, in the very beginning you are realistic, then the match has a better chance to succeed.

With Cancer, you have a tendency to try many things, to experiment. Eventually, you could come up with a money-making plan. It takes persistence. Cancer provides a steadying influence, especially where funds are concerned. If you are willing to overcome some of your wanderlust, then Cancer could be ideal. Cancer appreciates your sense of humor. You are drawn to Cancer because, in your eyes, these natives represent solidity.

Cancer stimulates you to think, to create. With Cancer, you can make money and valuable contacts. But it takes a mature Cancer—and a grown-up Gemini—for this relationship to last. Unless a special effort is made, the relationship could evaporate—by mutual consent.

Each is sensitive to the moods of the other. Depression proves catching. Constant dialogue is a necessity. Otherwise, minor misunderstandings grow out of proportion.

Cancer makes you security-conscious. You are less likely to speculate, more apt to go in for solid investments. You add to possessions—you spend to earn. You invest. Cancer helps you to understand land values, real estate. Cancer gives you a sense of pride in ownership.

In all, the relationship represents challenge. The effort could be worthwhile; but success in this association does not come on a silver platter. You must earn it.

Gemini with Leo

Leo persons fit into your general scheme—you are attracted to Leo, you are mentally stimulated by Leo and you would like to settle down and make a life with Leo. But, Gemini, Leo can be elusive. Very often Gemini and Leo get together to learn lessons from each other. Leo sets a fast pace and, Gemini, for once you are willing to slow down. But, alas, Leo is just getting started.

The signs are compatible. A sense of humor prevails in this relationship—lots of laughs. But laughter can become shrill and turn to tears. Unless you are willing to keep up, to read, to write, to travel, to make changes, then the harmony that prevails at the beginning could sour. Leo individuals inspire you, give you ideas, make you want to give of yourself. Many of your contacts and your romances are associated with Leo.

Domestic conditions can be at the center of your relationship with Leo. There is talk of common residence, marriage—you find, to a degree, peace and harmony with Leo. But, listen, Gemini: the chief result of this relationship is mental stimulation for you. Ideas are plentiful. But Leo tends to discipline you. Leo encourages you to be discriminating . . . to choose the best of many plans, schemes, ideas, possibilities.

Whether or not the Gemini-Leo relationship lasts, it does provide fireworks and plenty of heat. But, ideally, Gemini, you require *warmth.* And whether or not the heat will ultimately generate warmth depends on the degree of determination exercised by both Gemini and Leo.

The Sun of Leo and your Mercury blend to create a kind of stimulation which results in short journeys, heated disputes, separations and reconciliations. To put it mildly—plenty of action!

Gemini with Virgo

In connection with Virgo, these persons tend to restrict you, to bring home an awareness of responsibility. Virgo and Gemini share the same ruling planet, which is Mercury. Combined, this produces a relationship which smacks of *me first.* When you talk to Virgo, you don't listen. Instead, you half-listen while planning your answer or retort.

Virgo affects that part of your chart connected with home environment, stability and property. Virgo tends to correct you and slow you down. When done in a constructive, sympathetic manner, this is all to the good. The key, Gemini, is to choose a *mature Virgo.* Otherwise, there is conflict, even combat.

You have never been noted for choosing the right persons. But, when dealing with Virgo, realize that long-range projects could be at stake, as well as your future and such material things as property and home. When you play with Virgo, you are playing for keeps . . . and you had better not enter the game in the first place unless you are familiar with the rules, the regulations and the possible consequences.

Gemini and Virgo are drawn together by circumstances, by mutual interests affecting the security of both. Listen, Gemini: you do have lessons to learn from Virgo. But be sure you are ready before you enroll in the class.

The "double dose" of Mercury raises the question of who is to take the lead. Virgo wants to serve, to offer constructive criticism. You want action. Who says when to go, when to remain? That becomes a major point of contention in this relationship.

In all, Gemini and Virgo really have much in common; but the fact that friction exists between you cannot be denied.

Gemini with Libra

You relate to Libra in an exciting, creative sense. The signs Gemini and Libra are trined, or compatible. You are aroused physically by Libra. The area of your Solar horoscope associated with love, sex, affection, courtship and self-expression is touched by Libra. The Gemini-Libra combination equals Mercury and Venus, and the two signs together can make profound music.

Plainly, this is no relationship that can be laughed off, tampered with or taken as a lark. If you're not serious, Gemini, don't become involved with Libra. The stakes are too high, including children, affection, the very heartbeat of your being. You see, this is not the kind of association you turn on or off. Once on, the light burns brightly.

Once on, the heat generated leads forward, to complications, to involvement. We should repeat, perhaps; if you don't intend to get involved, don't start with Libra in the first place.

Listen, Gemini: you learn from Libra . . . you learn lessons of dedication and love. You learn to give, to exchange . . . and to receive graciously. It's very important to adhere to principles. Once you fall down on these, the relationship suffers.

The higher you set your sights, the better for both you and Libra. Your wonderful teaching and reporting qualities are stimulated by the relationship. Your creative resources are brought forward.

Children could have much to do with this relationship. Gemini and Libra are especially harmonious when dealing with youngsters. Basically, the relationship is healthy. The attraction is there—and it could, for you, represent basic fulfillment.

You may find Libra too placid. You may want Libra to possess more get-up-and-go. But the steadying influence here could be advantageous. Patience, Gemini, patience!

Gemini with Scorpio

With Scorpio you are intrigued, but the relationship can be a trying one. You tend to finish before you start, to envision such great projects that you are tired before you actually get going!

With Scorpio, you work. You try to break through but find yourself in a kind of maze. You run hither and yon, which is familiar to the Gemini nature. Scorpio touches that part of your chart associated with service, pets, employees, general health and jobs as differentiated from position or career. The Scorpio individual makes you aware of health and work resolutions—and regulations.

In connection with Scorpio, you become the person who helps, who aids those with problems. Usually, Gemini, it is you who confides in others. But Scorpio confides in you and, before you know it, you have promised to tackle a project. You begin working . . . and then you begin to rebel.

This is not an easy relationship because it might lack some of the excitement Gemini craves. There is a steadying influence; you can gain from it. But you have to be patient, and you must be dedicated. Scorpio makes you finish what you start. And this, in itself, is good. You see, Gemini, you do your best when you know that there is nowhere to go until a current cycle is completed, the job finished. With Scorpio, you get down to the business at hand—and you usually finish it.

Gemini needs at least one Scorpio. This is because natives of this sign serve your needs. You don't always know what it is you require—and Scorpio helps clarify this area. The Pluto of Scorpio, combined with your Mercury, enables you better to perceive long-range goals. You may change your mind, may take detours, but at least you do know where you ultimately are going.

Gemini with Sagittarius

Here is a case of opposites attracting each other; that's the way it is with Gemini and Sagittarius. The Jupiter of Sagittarius blends with your Mercury to signify responsibility, money, powerful emotions, intensified relations. Sagittarius can cheer you, stimulate ambition, help educate you and cause you to concentrate on a goal.

Sagittarius spotlights that part of your Solar horoscope related to marriage, contracts, legal affairs, partnerships and public relations. Natives of this sign touch that part of your chart related to the way the world looks to you. And, very often, Sagittarius looks attractive to you.

There are no halfway measures here; it is all the way or nothing. Once the knot is tied, once the relationship gets started, there are responsibilities and an air of permanency. The affairs of Gemini and Sagittarius intermingle. It definitely is not a matter of hit-and-run. Know this, Gemini, and act accordingly.

You can make money with Sagittarius. You gain authority through added responsibility. Sagittarius can help make you feel more secure. Sagittarius philosophizes; Gemini is active. These traits form a bond of attraction.

An association with Sagittarius could be serious business. It could lead to a commitment, to anything from a business contract, to a partnership, to marriage.

Sagittarius helps make you more optimistic. You see where you are headed—and can detect ultimate profit. Your days of aimless journey are over when you team with Sagittarius.

Gemini with Capricorn

Capricorn appeals to your sense of mystery and glamour. But money is involved and you must attend to details. You see, Gemini, Capricorn persons will not readily understand your restless nature. And they make demands. You are capable of fulfilling these demands . . . but this doesn't mean you will *want* to do so. It's not very easy for you to keep secrets from Capricorn. In a positive sense, Capricorn relieves you of burdens and helps get to the bottom of mysteries. In a negative sense, Capricorn merely gets under your skin.

You learn about yourself through a relationship with Capricorn. You dig deep, uncover mysteries, see a side of yourself which was not previously visible. Capricorn encourages you to seek investment opportunities. Capricorn can teach you to invest in your own talents. You gain through this association, Gemini, if you're willing to bear down—if you mean business. Capricorn will see through any halfway methods or half-hearted attempts.

The keynote of the relationship is money, responsibility and hidden assets. This may not be the most romantic combination, but there is drive here and certainly there is attraction.

Capricorn helps you get started and could be instrumental in providing a greater degree of financial security.

Listen, Gemini—if you need balance, if you desire a sense of well-being—then you have found the right individual in Capricorn.

The Saturn of Capricorn blends with your Mercury to provide a degree of discipline. Some of your freedom is curtailed. You learn to play the waiting game. With Capricorn, you learn to be observant. You dig for information beyond the superficial level. Capricorn teaches you to be thorough. With Capricorn, you handle the money of other people. You will have an interesting time, but the restrictions could become depressing.

Gemini with Aquarius

With Aquarius, you tend to be restless, almost as if you were associating with another Gemini. Aquarius touches that part of your Solar horoscope related to journeys, mental activity, publishing, writing, the ability to reach out and stretch above your environment. Aquarius persons stimulate you to learn and cause you to be dissatisfied with the status quo. The Uranus of Aquarius and your Mercury add up to a finalizing of desires. Aquarius leads you, always promising more—until you become rather exhausted from following and anticipating.

Uranus and Mercury respectively rule Gemini and Aquarius. This, in turn, points to a kind of mental acrobatics. You certainly will meet your match in Aquarius if you are seeking to be far out. You'll get a great companion and counterpart if you want to be on the move, to travel, to learn, to report and to record your findings.

Aquarius gets you going, stimulates you—and then may have a change of heart, a change of mind. Aquarius could represent something of a burden for you. Such an association means responsibility, but not necessarily any financial reward. Aquarius gets you interested in causes. You campaign and expend nervous energy. But, Gemini, when it's all over you may ask yourself, *"What do I have to show for it?"*

If it's excitement you seek, and a better understanding of the world in which you live, then don't hesitate to tie up with Aquarius. But if it's profit that is your motive, it's best to look elsewhere.

With Aquarius, you could embark upon long journeys. Uranus (Aquarius) and your Mercury blend to create progress. Interest in the welfare of others is emphasized. You create better conditions for others, but often at a sacrifice to yourself.

That's how it is likely to be when you team up with Aquarius. Overall, the match is beneficial. In any case, the excitement of self-discovery is featured.

Gemini with Pisces

Here, with Pisces, your career is affected. So are your ambitions, aspirations—and so, too, is your status. The Neptune of Pisces blends with Mercury, your ruling planet, to produce an element of confusion. Pisces puzzles you. There is an air of mystery about Pisces and you want to penetrate it. Neptune and Mercury can add up to creative imagination—or it can add up to deception.

The final answer depends, of course, upon the Pisces and Gemini individuals.

You, Gemini, are apt to reach out for perfection in this relationship. You want to advance, to gain authority and power. Pisces aids in this direction; but, very often, it is on Pisces' terms.

You may be deceived into thinking you can be the dominant one with Pisces. This will not be the case. Pisces, in a subtle manner, leads the way. You eventually could become an unwilling follower!

There are problems here; there is also an abundance of romantic feeling. But the romance could lack staying power; it is not so much passion as it is anticipation. In a way, your relationship with Pisces is akin to chasing a rainbow. It seems within grasp, but somehow proves evasive. The relationship seems nebulous and on the brink. There is desire. There is also illusion. Turning illusion to reality is the task to be accomplished if the relationship is to succeed.

Pisces could drive you and demand an accounting of your accomplishments; this might build resentment. It is fine for the fulfillment of certain ambitions, but takes much will power if it is to result in a lasting partnership.

Gemini and Pisces learn from each other—and the lessons could be difficult ones. If, Gemini, you're just out for a lark, you could get your wings clipped.

Cancer

June 21 - July 22

As you are quite aware, the moods of others have a direct effect on your own emotions. This carries over into the area of sex. In your sexual pattern or activities, you tend to blend. Perhaps a better way of stating this is to say that you bend! Which means, Cancer, that you concentrate on giving rather than receiving pleasure.

On the surface, this may appear noble. To a certain extent, it is commendable. Carried to extremes, it could upset an otherwise healthy relationship. To become so receptive that you no longer provide any challenge is to invite difficulty.

Sex is a powerful drive; without it there would cease to be life. I realize this is more of a cliché than a profound statement. But, with you, it is necessary to emphasize the power, the challenge of sex—and, too, the sheer joy of it.

Too often, where you are concerned, the joy, the satisfaction and the gratification are felt by the other half. Where Leo can be a selfish lover, where others can be lazy lovers, you tend to be one who acquiesces, who seeks to please—and this can result in a one-sided relationship.

The *giving* rather than the *receiving* of pleasure could create a dilemma. If your partner is one whose ego requires the satisfaction of knowing that he or she has *provided* satisfaction, your pattern is going to be a problem. This kind of partner, with sexual ego, is not going to be happy if you acquiesce too much—this kind of partner will want you to receive as well as give. And that is a lesson astrology teaches you in this area: it is necessary to receive as well as to give. That's your basic sexual lesson, Cancer.

Your sexual urge is strong, very much a part of your life. Recognize this and receive as well as give satisfaction. Be willing to tear down old habit patterns; tear down in order to rebuild.

You cherish affection. Protection of family and loyalty to loved ones are a basic part of your makeup. But, Cancer, when loyalty creates "blind spots," adjustment to reality is required. Your loyalty can be of the blind variety. Your giving or bending could lead you in aimless circles. In turn, this could prevent you from fully participating in a relationship—no matter how much you tell yourself that you are pleased, satisfied, loved and loving.

It is necessary for you, where sex is concerned, to become more of an individual—with individual needs, desires, foibles. This is essential if you are to achieve real fulfillment. Your Cancer Moon represents the feminine principle. Thus, the tendency is for you to "mother" your lover (whether you are male or female). This could create a kind of maternal relationship rather than an exciting exchange between two mature, loving adults.

On the positive side, you are all that a partner could ask—warm, giving, responding to the touch of love. This is the challenge: to be positive, to break from old, outmoded concepts and to rebuild on knowledge, intelligence, sensitivity—on the realization that *you must be pleased in order to please in return.*

Cancer women are lovely and often lonely. They reach out for affection and love. But if their desire for security is not fulfilled, they could stray. You are a seeker. When unhappy in your sexual pattern, you could give in to curiosity, longing. This can lead to a greater lack of security—to more straying, and eventually it could lead to emotional disaster. A word of advice: *Be satisfied*—even if you have to tear down some illusions and face harsh realities.

Cancer men are emotional, sensitive to surroundings. The sex act, for the Cancer man, is not something he regards as separate or singular: it is connected with home, surroundings—and even good food! The Cancer man stands as a living example of "the way to a man's heart is through his stomach." At least, that's likely to be the case with the male Cancer. If this man is not pleased with his partner's culinary efforts, there is apt to be a hangover of dissatisfaction in the conjugal area. Why this should be is not our task to delineate. It is a psychological trait identifiable with the classic Cancer man. It *is.* That's what's important.

On a more negative level, the Cancer man clutters up his sexual life. These men born under Cancer become so involved with security, self-doubts, wonder and worry over home, food, business, that the vital sexual relationship is diminished by comparison.

Man or woman, born under this zodiacal sign, you have a tendency to attract clandestine relationships. The sign on the cusp of your Fifth, or sex House, is Scorpio. This enables us to obtain a clear picture of this side of your life; it is one of deep involvement. And you must keep your guard up or that beloved security of yours could go down the drain. Unscrupulous individuals are apt to play on your sympathies . . . to flatter you . . . to cook for you . . . to wine you and dine you . . . to dazzle and "hypnotize" you . . . and, before you know it, you are involved in a secret love affair.

Through it all, however, your practical nature remains. If an affair of the heart is finished, you are capable of adjusting—or readjusting. You seldom give up something for nothing. You possess a healthy curiosity concerning sex. At times, it is difficult to know whether your drive is dictated by passion . . . or curiosity.

You are idealistic; your desire is for sex to lead to home and security. Yet, there is an air of mystery which clings; you want to delve into the unknown. If your partner makes the predictable moves, if love-making deteriorates into mere routine, your ardor cools. Then, Cancer, that "straying" element could come to the fore.

Getting down to cases: your sex drive is strong. But it is not necessarily an end in itself. It is, more likely, a *means to an end.* This is not to state that you are conniving in this area. But it is to indicate that your view is far-reaching. Being intimate, where you are concerned, involves the trappings of hearth and home. Without these, as at least prospects, your drives tend to dissolve.

In sex, as in other areas, your twin adversaries are jealousy and possessiveness. I continue to point out to you, Cancer, that once you learn to let go, life becomes more of a song than a dirge. If this can be implanted in your subconscious, your success will be enhanced.

You regard marriage as an adventure, one which includes sex. There is also a sense of restriction and responsibility in your attitude toward marriage. You tend to attract a marriage partner who tests you, challenges you, encourages you to be an innovator—you attract one who changes your way of life.

Where sex is concerned, you tend to attract opposites—that is, someone who might be regarded as the opposite of your character makeup. It is you who usually makes adjustments. This you are prepared to do; but the conditions must be favorable and you must also feel you are involved with the right individual.

Sex, where you are concerned, can become a means of changing habits, of renovating a way of life. You are not apt to stand still once involved in an affair of the heart. Now, the line between change, versatility—and experimentation—is a fine one. You will not be happy if you are promiscuous. This is not a lecture on morals. Being a Cancer, you can understand the practical side of this problem. You simply do not acclimate to looseness. The variety, the experimentation, the adventure of sex, where your happiness is at stake, usually involves a one-and-only.

Your eye roves more than do you; your curiosity is healthy. But, when the chips are down, you usually live up to commitments. You are sensitive enough to realize the havoc that can be caused by indiscriminate sexual activity.

You're no angel. But neither are you a person who breaks vows, who shatters homes, who throws aside security for temporary thrill. Before you commit yourself, you exhibit a tendency to be inconstant. You are not being flighty; you just do not enter lightly into what could be a permanent relationship.

Sex, for you, involves various areas; these include home, family, and general *acceptance* of your partner. Which, perhaps, is another way of stating that you, more so than with most persons, must *respect* your partner if proper responses are to be forthcoming.

When love does not go well, you turn to food. And because your body tends to, retain liquid, an unhappy love affair could result in added poundage. It is a fact, Cancer, that love and food are almost interchangeable with you. If relations with the opposite sex are constructive and you are happy, your figure, general tone and appearance reflect that contentment. When unhappy, you eat without enjoying it; you eat merely to compensate—and the weight problem arises.

This can be somewhat of a vicious circle; when love goes sour, food becomes sweet. Then your appearance is less attractive—and there is less chance of success on the rebound. Cancer, when you feel good, you look good. Know this; *look good* and you will attract conditions that result in a good feeling. Of course, this is easier to say than to do. It requires discipline on your part. Knowing that your emotional welfare is at stake, you should he able to handle the problem wisely.

It boils down to: *look good, feel good.* Control your appetite; moderation is the key. So easy to say! But, Cancer, it is said to you because you possess innate wisdom in these matters. You have a sense of protection; you know how to do things for your own good. In the sexual area, this knowledge is invaluable. In all, sex is a powerful urge; in you, the drive is accented. To be less than happy in this area is to invite related problems. It isn't necessary; you can be contented. You need not turn to excesses as the result of a setback; you need not take the lid off eating and drinking. You can keep your appearance attractive, despite any emotional wound. And if you do, the wound heals, the experience nourishes, and you are on the road to another chance for happiness.

You tie up sex with family, home, and domesticity; it is, where you are concerned, a continuous link. In some instances, this is constructive. In others, it could be a misconception. Flexibility is essential for you in matters of sex: versatility of attitude. You make yourself a less exciting person if bogged down with one and only one attitude: that sex must be linked to family and home. That is an eventuality; it is not the necessary beginning and end. This is emphasized because, Cancer, it is likely to be one of your hang-ups. The sex area is important; it is not easy to delineate. But, in your case, there are some obvious lessons. For one, you should learn that sex and reproduction are not necessarily the same.

Dr. Mary Calderone seemed to be directing her remarks at the Cancer native when she declared:

"Reproduction and sex are not the same thing; nor can one equate sex and sexuality." The good doctor was pointing out that attitude has much to do with happiness in this area. Knowledge is not enough. It is your attitude toward what you know that counts. And this is especially significant for you, Cancer.

You must not bury your pleasure principle. When you do, the price is paid through excessive weight or other problems. You can be responsible, discriminating, loyal, without shutting the door to sexual fulfillment.

For you, an element of mystery is necessary for sexual pleasure. You cannot expect to have everything planned or itemized and still be able to emanate from your being a kind of sexuality which causes your partner to dedicate himself to your pleasure. Throw away the catalog! Abandon notions about what is and what is not necessary. Replace them with what is *good,* joyous, satisfying. Then, Cancer, you look good, feel good—you will *be* good.

How You Relate to the Other Signs

Cancer is harmonious in relation to Taurus, Virgo, Scorpio and Pisces. Your sign is not favorably aspected to Aries, Libra or Capricorn. Cancer can be considered neutral where the following signs are concerned: Leo, Sagittarius, Aquarius and Gemini.

Scorpio individuals attract you in a physical sense. Pisces persons heighten your ideals and stimulate your curiosity. But just as Pisces and Scorpio natives attract you, so does any person who is stimulating, imaginative, and who is not foolish where issues of money and security are concerned.

Of course, the above represents the briefest view of how you relate to the other zodiacal signs. There are further details, nuances, and indications. Let's elaborate on some of the highlights.

Cancer with Aries

Your sign, Cancer, gets a career boost from an association with Aries. Natives of Aries affect that part of your Solar horoscope connected with prestige, career, and ambitions. The Mars of Aries acts as an electric charge; you Set going, you quicken the pace, you sell, you drive, you declare yourself "in the race." Aries is not well aspected to your sign. But Aries, nevertheless, can help set you up in business. Aries can show you how to utilize your assets.

At times, Aries sets too fast a pace; this causes you to become apprehensive. You want to be sure of security; you check before taking a major step. But, with Aries, you are in business, an entrepreneur. Your standing in the community rises; your ambitions become realities. Yet, with all this potential, there is emotional conflict. A major conflict could arise where your home is concerned. Aries might choose one place, one area; you could select something entirely different. The fiery temperament of Aries and the receptivity of the Water element of your sign do not mix. The relationship succeeds on all fronts only if both Aries and Cancer are mature. Also, if other aspects between the charts (requiring horoscope comparison) are harmonious. Basically, the relationship could spark activity, but could also end up as a flash in the pan.

Aries and Cancer become impatient with each other. You find that Aries encourages you one minute, then offers criticism. If you are a woman, an Aries man will help you attain commercial success. There is also a degree of physical attraction, although it is not overwhelming. If you are a Cancer man, the Aries woman could nag you until you better your position in life.

You can both—Cancer and Aries—exhibit a stubborn streak. Neither one is an angel. And you could certainly learn from each other. If you feel adventurous, Cancer, give it a try!

Cancer with Taurus

With Taurus, a genuine friendship can ensue. But Taurus could also encourage an extravagant streak in you. Taurus is an individual you want to impress. In so doing, you go all out—you spend time and money. Taurus is well aspected to your sign, Cancer, but you must know when to get down to business. Otherwise, the relationship can become one of all play, no work. Then you become resentful of lost time and money, you sulk, you become moody.

This can be avoided if you learn to balance business and pleasure. Taurus has lessons to teach you. If you observe, you learn. But if you merely accept and put in time, there is not much to be gained.

In connection with a Taurus individual, you could find yourself going in circles. You start here and end up at the beginning. Which means, Cancer, *you* will have to provide the sense of direction. Taurus persons affect that part of your chart having to do with pleasure, aspirations, and friendships. There can also be a strong physical attraction. Although you meet people through Taurus, you are apt to end up ultimately being interested solely in Taurus; which leaves you right back where you started in the first place.

Your Moon and the Venus of Taurus could add up to romance. You *appreciate* each other. More important, you are each tolerant of the foibles of the other. There is mutual respect inherent in this relationship. It is evident, Cancer, that many of your dreams, hopes and wishes could be fulfilled through a close association with one born under Taurus.

Cancer with Gemini

Clandestine affairs, mystery, and intrigue are featured when you get together with Gemini. Some of your secret desires in this area can be fulfilled by Gemini. With Gemini, a kind of storybook romance ensues; the secret meeting, the pacts, the promises, the broken appointments, the misunderstandings, the coincidences which seem to occur when people are intimate.

The signs are regarded as neutral in relation to each other, but the Gemini Mercury and your Moon ruler can create an atmosphere of subdued tension. Gemini affects that part of your Solar horoscope associated with institutions, restrictions, and secrets. You tend to confide in Gemini persons. You find them interesting because, by some means, they cause you to look inward.

Gemini has a tendency to shake you up. The relationship could proceed on promises . . . or could burst as if a fragile bubble. Plainly, there is a lack of reality in this association; you are charmed by Gemini animation. But you may find it difficult to pin down these persons.

You gain through Gemini if activity is associated with raising funds for charitable organizations. That's the general pattern; what you get is not personal profit. With your awareness of money and property, you would find Gemini a kind of luxury rather than a necessity.

There is a tendency for Gemini and Cancer to criticize each other. The two persons care for each other and, thus, are seeking to correct faults. But, invariably, an eroding takes place; the relationship tends to grow thin.

If it is a secret romance you seek, Cancer, then you have found the right individual. But, for practical purposes, Gemini may not fill the bill.

Cancer with Cancer

With another Cancer, the association tends to get tied down with red tape. It is not the most exciting relationship. Two Cancer individuals are apt to find much to criticize about each other.

The Cancer woman needs to share your life, not merely wait on you. She needs assurance and reassurance. If you want this woman to be your lover, you have to let her know she is loved. If you do, the result will be an exciting, satisfying relationship.

This woman demands sincerity and an abundance of affection. She is feminine; she is, above all else, a woman. She is also practical. If you intend only to take, you will lose her. If you give as well as receive, she will be strongly attached to you. If you deceive her, she has the sixth sense to uncover the deception—and to unload you.

A Cancer man will let you spoil him to the point of no return—if you so permit it. A good meal is satisfying to him, but he wants to know that the food was prepared with an ingredient of love.

He has much to offer, but he doesn't give easily. You must make him aware, from the beginning, that his relationship with you is to be an equal partnership—give and take. He makes numerous demands, because he thinks (often rightly so) that he's worth it. He is affectionate, needs to know you'll be there when he needs you. In turn, have him realize that you have some needs and some requirements of your own. Do so without being tough. A gentle, loving approach is a winning one. He will value the relationship more when he understands how much you value yourself.

Cancer with Leo

There's much attraction in this combination; also, Leo is apt to brighten your financial picture. Your Moon combines with the Leo Sun significator to make life interesting. There are enough differences to create healthy curiosity. The relationship is not apt to be dull.

Leo affects that part of your chart related to income, money, and personal possessions. You accumulate additional goods with Leo. This makes it necessary to stimulate income potential. And this you can do when combining forces with natives of Leo. Your horizons broaden; you have an interest in obtaining the better things in life.

Leo can be obstinate; you are protective. The relationship is not problem-free; there are obstacles. It is probably going to be necessary, Cancer, for you to play the receptive role while Leo is dominant. This does not mean you should be dominated. But you probably will be the one to give ground if the relationship is to last.

Leo is fascinated by you; the feeling in Leo, where you are concerned, is one of fear mingled with security. Your feelings are more clearly defined; you sense that Leo can provide you with necessities and lead you on to glitter and gold. You may have to permit Leo to chase you until you catch him.

Social life improves when you combine forces with lively Leo. A key word is *expansion.* You do not stand still with Leo; there is travel, study, writing, advertising, self-expression. Leo could tire you—but you won't be bored.

Leo needs praise, while you require security. These elements can be successfully combined, provided both you and Leo are mature—and sincere.

Cancer with Virgo

Virgo persons affect that part of your chart related to journeys, relatives, ideas, restlessness. The combination of Virgo's Mercury and your significator, the Moon, makes for plans, for ideas, for a desire to experiment. On the negative side, Cancer and Virgo cook up half-baked schemes. On a positive level, Virgo stimulates you mentally and some genuine progress could result. Virgo individuals make you think, and analyze. But, Cancer, you tend to seek perfection here. Virgo prods. Virgo criticizes. Virgo is aware of health, of work, employment. And if you intend to live a life of ease, you had better look elsewhere. Virgo doesn't let down easily. There is apt to be a steady flow of pressure.

Virgo makes you aware of rivals, of competition. Virgo causes you to be dissatisfied with existing conditions. The two signs are well aspected, but you get along best with Virgo if you do more *listening* than asserting.

Virgo could irritate you through constant striving toward improvement. Virgo will try to change your diet. Virgo will urge you to see this specialist, that one—and yet another. You will embark on numerous short journeys while relating to Virgo.

There is stimulation here, but the ties need cementing or they snap. It might be best for you to choose a Virgo who is older. Otherwise, the pace, the movement, the changes, the appointments, could prove tiring and contribute to frayed nerves.

The Moon-Mercury combination can best be described as *brittle.* Virgo loves doing things for you. But you may find it difficult to pin Virgo down; just when you are ready to settle down, Virgo is on the move. The biggest problem is likely to be deciding how and where to live.

Virgo admires you, is more than mildly interested—and this admiration and interest serve as a stimulus for you. If, Cancer, you don't expect perfection, and can put up with some friendly criticism, then Virgo is for you.

Cancer with Libra

With Libra, you become concerned with security, with your position later in life. Libra makes you aware of investments, savings programs, home, and solid structures. Libra gives you a solid frame of reference which you can understand. This relationship, however, could get bogged down in a kind of work pattern which does not nourish you in other directions.

In association with Libra, you become security-conscious. You gain a degree of stability, because Libra affects that part of your chart. Your Fourth Solar House is emphasized by Libra—this is connected with domestic surroundings, home, property, land and the foundation for a prosperous future.

Generally, there are obstacles to this relationship. Libra *churns your apprehensions*—makes you so aware of the need to build that you could despair of ever accomplishing your goal.

But, Cancer, if you are ready to settle down . . . if ready to concentrate on home and family . . . then you may have found the right person in Libra.

A thorough understanding is required before coming seriously involved. With you and Libra, that understanding comes about through a dialogue. You can't take things for granted with Libra. Everything has to be direct and on the line. Do some thinking and analyzing, state your conclusions to Libra, then *evaluate* the reaction.

The Venus significator of Libra combines with your Moon indicator to suggest material success. Certainly, your portfolio of stocks could grow, if this holds your interest. With Libra, the aim is toward having something ready for tomorrow.

But you are apt to be so well prepared for tomorrow that you miss living today. That's one of the problems of a relationship between Cancer and Libra. Understand and perceive—if wise and determined, you could make it work.

Cancer with Scorpio

With Scorpio, there is physical attraction. Scorpio natives touch that part of your chart relating to love, to excitement, to speculation, to children, to courtship, to change, to variety—and adventure. There is plenty of compatibility between you and Scorpio. But *don't play games.* This relationship is likely to be for keeps where Scorpio is concerned. Know this and act accordingly.

There is the warmth of attraction here—and the sparks easily ignite into a roaring flame. With Scorpio, there is change—and you soon come out of any shell. Listen, Cancer; realize you are attracted to Scorpio. Accept that as a cold fact. Don't attempt to rationalize. But, along the same line, don't misinterpret the attraction for anything else.

The attraction gets Cancer and Scorpio together. How you build from there is another story. But what I am trying to say, Cancer, is this: just because there is an attraction does not mean you will live happily ever after. That depends on the maturity of Cancer, of Scorpio—that depends on how your complete charts blend.

Basically, the two signs harmonize. You will have to be the receptive one—Scorpio presses, is forceful and dominant. If you are wise, and if you want the attraction to grow into something permanent, take appropriate steps. Utilize your innate wisdom, Cancer. If you do this, Scorpio indeed can be for you.

The Pluto significator of Scorpio, combined with your Moon ruler, adds up to physical warmth. Scorpio helps you pursue creative endeavors. The relationship is a powerful one; it builds steam. Unless there is a constructive outlet, an explosion occurs. Scorpio is especially good for you when dealing with children. Scorpio helps you tap creative resources, aids you in understanding emotions, including those of the primitive variety. If you can't stand the heat, though, don't mingle with Scorpio.

Cancer with Sagittarius

Sagittarius performs vital services for you. The Jupiter of Sagittarius combines with your Moon to encourage expansion, the tackling of assignments which keep you busy and represent a definite challenge. Sagittarius affects that part of your chart related to health, work, pets, employment, service. Sagittarius can make life more convenient for you.

Listen: Sagittarius is not as exciting, where you are concerned, as is Scorpio. But the relationship could be more pleasant. Scorpio excites you physically and could cause you to work yourself into a frenzy. Sagittarius is concerned about your health, about making you comfortable.

Natives of Sagittarius have a way of helping you to relax. You get basic tasks completed, but without strain. There is, however, a lack of fire here. With Sagittarius you investigate, try various projects. But the staying power may not be too great. You tend, in this relationship, to lapse into a sort of benign attitude. On the negative side, you begin taking Sagittarius for granted; you expect to be served, cajoled. In turn, Sagittarius comes to depend on you in a financial sense. Thus, Cancer and Sagittarius fulfill mutual needs, but the tie may not be binding.

The Jupiter of Sagittarius comforts you; you feel there is more to accomplish, additional places to see, a multiplicity of experiences to encounter. This ultimately, however, could create a vacuum where satisfaction is concerned. "What's next" could become your refrain with Sagittarius.

The mixture here could separate before it jells; knowing this, enter the relationship with a sense of awareness. If you do this, success could crown the mutual efforts of Cancer and Sagittarius.

Cancer with Capricorn

You break from routine in relationship with Capricorn. The accent here is on partnership, marriage, public relations. Capricorn brings you out of yourself. The Saturn of Capricorn combines with your Moon significator to stress independence, originality, and new experiences. You are attracted to Capricorn—but much in the manner that opposites attract each other.

Capricorn inspires confidence; you are able to break from the status quo. With Capricorn, you combine efforts, interests; the relationship could lead to marriage.

You gain not only confidence with Capricorn, but also a greater sense of responsibility. You aim at achievement. Capricorn can cause you to be dissatisfied with what you have; you aim for greater heights. Capricorn makes you aware of the public, of reaction to your efforts. With Capricorn, you are not likely to maintain the same habit patterns. You see the new; you want to test your skills. You seek plaudits, approval. Where previously you might have settled in one niche, you now strive to break down barriers. That's the effect Capricorn is likely to have on you.

Cancer and Capricorn may have opposing views. But it could happen that both change—and both discover new interests. If this occurs, Capricorn and Cancer can grow together. And, of course, this would make an ideal situation and create a fine relationship.

Both signs have an innate desire for security. Yet, working together, they are willing to take a chance on new ideas, new projects. They could make excellent business partners.

With Capricorn, if you're both mature, you could find constructive outlets for the desire to give and receive, to serve and be rewarded; you could fan an inner flame that lights future prospects.

Cancer with Aquarius

There is a kind of warmth here; attraction exists and you are drawn to natives of Aquarius. Harmony could prevail, if financial problems are overcome. Aquarius touches that part of your chart related to the occult, the hidden, to the money of partners, to the financial situation of others: money is a definite part of the picture—and so is mystery.

You are intrigued by natives of this sign; you feel they have the answers to mysteries. You confide in Aquarians; this includes intimate matters. Aquarius stimulates your interest in the occult. Although you desire security, you are receptive to ideas that are unorthodox. Aquarius highlights this part of your nature. And Aquarius causes you to visualize domestic harmony based on a tie of real affection. Although you are more directly attracted to Scorpio, in a physical sense, you also are drawn to Aquarius. With Scorpio, you *know* the *reason* for the attraction; with Aquarius, the attraction is there, but it is not always obvious.

Going into partnership with Aquarius could prove profitable. Whatever the relationship, it tends to evolve around possessions, profit, mutual benefits, interests, even marriage. If you're married to one who is not an Aquarian, your mate could have financial dealings with Aquarius.

With Aquarius, there is concentration upon material goods. Also, there is an emphasis on home and harmony in the domestic area. You are able to help Aquarius find profitable means of self-expression. And the relationship could prove mutually profitable.

The Uranus of Aquarius combines with your Moon Significator to produce a sense of adventure. With Aquarius, you *could* strike it rich—in more ways than one.

Cancer with Pisces

You enjoy traveling with a Pisces individual. Pisces touches that part of your chart related to journeys, including journeys of the mind. Learning becomes an adventure. Both Cancer and Pisces are Water Signs and well aspected to each other. A great deal of sympathy exists, but the two of you tend to get into a rut of gloom. This happens when your ideals are not fulfilled. Together, Pisces and Cancer may want to change the world—overnight.

Knowing this, Cancer, don't rush things. Read, study, be perceptive and subtle. *And don't try to boss the*

Piscean. Pisces may appear weak, but when you push too hard, Pisces rebels.

Pisces is good for you when it comes to expressing views in written form. Pisces helps you to publish, to advertise, to gain a wider audience for your creative efforts.

Your intuitive intellect is sparked by Pisces. And, Cancer, your ability to perceive trends is also heightened. You are a naturally sensitive individual—and in association with Pisces this sensitivity could express itself *through extrasensory perception.* Which means you seem to know, seem to sense what is going to occur. Trust your hunches when Pisces is around.

The Neptune of Pisces combines with your Moon significator to accent inspiration, spirituality—and, at times, a complete lack of practicality. With Pisces, your view is far-reaching: you are concerned with philosophy, with the way people who are far away think and live. Your horizons are broadened; you could take an overseas journey in the company of Pisces.

The relationship is favorable, though at times it could lack solidity. The Moon-Neptune combination is a romantic one; there is an abundance of idealism. But the blending here could be woven with gossamer threads.

Leo

July 23 - August 22

Sex, for you, is equated with a break from the ordinary, with a tearing down in order to rebuild; it is expansion, and represents pleasure and appreciation. Sex also could mean restriction. You tend to become intimate with those below your station—those who could curb other activities. In effect, sex for you can be gratifying, but there is apt to be sacrifice on other levels, mental or social or professional.

The Fifth House represents sex. Your Fifth Solar House is Sagittarius, signified by Jupiter. This combines with your Sun ruler to produce great expectations. At times, the expectations surpass the results.

As in many other areas, you are an idealist here. When your partner disappoints you in intelligence, actions, motives or aspirations, the intimacy is apt to lose its glow and become tarnished. If this happens, it results in ultimate disappointment.

Listen, Leo: you want the limelight, want the center of attention. But, with all of this, you can be plagued with the fear that you will not be quite able to live up to advance notices. You are creative and excited by all aspects of creativity, including sex. You need love: your "food" is affection. You are excellent at what sexologists term love play. But partners of Leo have been known to cornplain that, at times, the play has too long a run, and that when the curtain should go up on the real drama, the life-giving drama, Leo is so tired from the play that little is left for the main attraction.

You are impulsive and impetuous. If you're not mature, being admired becomes a fetish. You fall in love with love rather than with your partner. You perform rather than actually give of yourself. You are attractive to the opposite sex; on the negative side, this could suffice. You become more interested in the chase than in the catch. On a positive level, you are warm, generous, giving, and passionate in your desire to please a loved one.

Success in this area has much to do with intelligence. Respect for the intelligence of your partner plays a paramount role. Jupiter, associated with your own Fifth Sector (sex) symbolizes higher education, expansion, the reaching out for knowledge. It is not wrong to say, in your case, that you are first mentally attracted to an individual and that other kinds of attraction follow.

If this kind of respect for intelligence is not present, you tend to become dominating. You block off feelings of sensitivity. Your partner becomes an object rather than someone who is meaningful to you, someone who affects your emotions to the point where love becomes more than a word.

The key is to find someone whom you do respect, intellectually and otherwise. The problem is that, very often, you attract the other kind. You attract people who seem to want to be dominated. This represents the traditional vicious circle. It's important to pull yourself out of this pattern if indeed you have fallen into it. Otherwise, Leo, you deny yourself the happiness that comes from an exciting, mutual kind of pleasure available where two mature adults are involved.

You attract numerous affairs of the heart. The drama intrigues you. It is as though you were another individual, an objective one, looking on—viewing a play. When you truly mature, you will become *involved.* Not as a bystander, an onlooker—but as a true participant. You will throw off superficiality in favor of a basic, earthy relationship which, in its turn, sees you become more of a person, coming to terms with yourself, facing the music of life and love.

Both men and women of Leo have great expectations where love is concerned. When you find the right partner, life takes on an incandescent glow; there is warmth, security and the nourishment which comes as the result of engaging in a creative process.

Men and women of Leo tend, at times, to smother loved ones. You want to be adored, revered—you want your partner to gasp with excitement at almost every gesture. If this is not controlled, or overcome in the process of maturing, it creates a problem. You demand so much that you defeat your own purpose. In demanding, you often cause your partner to become "gun-shy." This causes a shriveling process—which is the opposite of what you actually desire.

Now, listen: challenge is fine and can be constructive. But challenge is also tense. Learn to appreciate the state of relaxation that results from physical-emotional fulfillment.

You are a pedestal builder; where loved ones are concerned, that is where you would like them to be—up there, so high at times that they are out of sight. This kind of idealism, Leo, is not constructive. When you find that a loved one is made of flesh and blood, you experience a letdown. Strive to overcome this "pedestal" tendency.

Sagittarius is the sign that has the most direct effect on you as far as physical attraction is concerned. Your own sign, Leo, is the natural fifth zodiacal sector. You and sex should not be strangers; afffection and love are as much a part of you as your hands and feet. You are warm, need attention, personal care, *tender lovning care.* You have no fondness for being alone. However, your impulsive nature sometimes takes the form of a temper tantrum—this, obviously, could cause you to be alone. If not in a temper, then you do foolish things, say things you do not really mean and, in general, do much to assure yourself of a state you have no desire to possess: the *state of loneliness.*

Now, listen: on the positive side, your desires are reciprocated, affection is returned, you are cared for and you are fulfilled. So, Leo, the obvious answer to any dilemma is to stop being negative!

As a Leo, man or woman, you want to be admired, looked up to, and appreciated, especially where sex is concerned. You need, also, to be reassured constantly. When your feelings are fully aroused, you give your all. You expose your emotions. Once that trust is abused, however, you harbor resentment that is difficult, if not impossible, to erase.

You want so much to attract the perfect mate that you can overlook one who would be harmonious. You seek afar, when in actuality what you need could be close at hand. You long for what is distant. What is available could lose its appeal. It is in this way that you display immaturity.

If, Leo, you are to gain contentment, you must be willing to lock horns with the here and now, not with the far away or long ago. You cherish romantic memories. Your habit patterns get fixed; what you had and lost is apt to be more cherished than what is now available.

You are not underhanded. As a matter of fact, you often wear your heart on your sleeve. You invite envy, jealousy. Yet you want to be the ruler, the dominating influence, the light of life, the lover's lover. You enjoy being waited on.

You could become a lazy lover; where you want your partner to be romantic, you want merely to be pleased. This could create a dilemma. You want love when you want it, but it would be wiser also to consider the needs, moods and desires of your partner.

Listen: you require an outlet for your emotions. You are quite dependent on affection. Without it, out goes your appetite, even your *appetite for living.* Loving is living for you—and you fall in and out of love. Unlike Gemini, however, you usually love one person at a time.

Your desire for approval is enormous. Avoid being overbearing and you are more likely to gain the approval you so sorely seek. You would rather be considered a great lover than an intellectual. Or, better, you envision yourself as a combination of both! Very often, Leo, you live up to your own expectations—you can be so much in love and out of love. However, you exhibit a tendency to be wasteful, extravagant with your talents, and affection. Self-control and thoughtfulness in this area can make you a happier person.

It seems that you often battle against being happy, although you want so much to find fulfillment. Get rid of that long-ago, far-away complex. It is all right to be in love with love, but it is not healthy to assume that what you have is, somehow, not what you need. This only leads to a merry-go-round of discontentment, bitterness, and self-pity.

Now, listen: sex for you can be a fulfilling experience. It can lead to happiness and make loneliness a stranger. But for this to happen, you will have to be involved to the extent that you care. Being involved in the popular sense, having an affair, is not the same. Emotional involvement, to the point of sacrificing your own luxuries, is required. Only then, can love find a way through the misty haze with which you unconsciously attempt to block happiness.

Forget yourself! Lose yourself in the needs of another. Don't be so concerned with appearances, pride, with being a "winner." Then, Leo, you will have touched a button which arouses emotions, which assures you of companionship, admiration, sex—and love.

How You Relate to the Other Signs

Leo is harmonious in relation to Gemini, Libra, Aries and Sagittarius. Leo is unfavorably aspected to Aquarius, Taurus or Scorpio. Leo is generally neutral in relation to Cancer, Virgo, Capricorn and Pisces.

You are drawn to humor and intelligence: Gemini often fills that role. You love a mystery, are fond of intrigue, and Cancer often fills that role. You prefer gentleness to a rough approach, and Libra often fills that need. You need a partner who is intellectual as well as physically attractive, and Aries could meet those requirements where you are concerned. You see, Leo, there actually is no need to be lonely if a desire from within is brought to the fore and that pride of yours can be confined rather than permitted to spread and engulf you.

Of course, the above represents the briefest view of how you relate to the other zodiacal signs. There are further details, nuances, indications. Let's elaborate on some of the highlights.

Leo with Aries

Aries touches that part of your Solar horoscope related to long journeys, philosophy, publishing, communications. The signs are well aspected; together, Aries and Leo represent originality, independence, a new approach.

This Mars of Aries, with your Sun, spells action. You could burn up with activity. The key is to outline the sense of direction, to know *where* you are going. Obviously, Aries spurs you to greater efforts, and is instrumental in gaining recognition for your efforts. There is also physical attraction here. But there could be a tendency to go too fast. In so doing, there could be mishaps.

You can, with Aries, articulate constructive ideas. Aries gains recognition and publicity for you. Aries flatters you—and when anyone does this, you are won over.

Aries is favorable, but tires you. You have to keep on your toes. You want to impress Aries. You may overextend yourself. There is only so much you can do. And, with Aries, you want to do it all.

With Aries, you would be wise to order a new supply of vitamins! The Mars of Aries and your Sun could catch fire, burn energy—and the need is for replacement, for reserve strength. Unless you understand this, there could be too much of a good thing.

Aries is especially helpful at aiding you to get ideas off the ground. You gain by strengthening your personal philosophy. Publishing enterprises are also aided by your association with Aries. Your views gain a wider audience.

A good relationship, Leo—*if* you take time out to catch your breath!

Leo with Taurus

With Taurus, you tend to get bogged down. The goal is there, it is visible, clear—but you can get sidetracked. Taurus tends to make you stick to routine, to get the job done from the bottom up. But, Leo, you often want to take the other route—to finish from the *top to the bottom.* Naturally, there is apt to be conflict. Taurus keeps an eye on the budget. You want to spend with the idea that all experience ultimately is worthwhile. But Taurus wants the cards on the table, face up. Taurus wants to see, to feel, to be specific. You take the overall view—and, with Taurus, a compromise is made which tends to water down any so-called master plan.

Listen, Leo: you need a Taurus to keep you striving toward goals, to elevate your standing in the community and in your professional endeavors. But you must utilize your natural fire and drive—and not permit it to be buried. With Taurus, the key is to achieve a balance between practicality and creativeness. This is not necessarily easy. But dealing with a Taurean isn't easy for everyone, especially Leos.

Avoid fooling yourself. Don't try to reform the Taurean, or force him to do things your way. If you do, there is conflict and little else. With Taurus, be patient. Taurus is stubborn—so is Leo. Together the combination is interesting, but might not get off the ground. However, if it does, then there is every likelihood that both will benefit.

The Taurus Venus combines with your Sun significator to create mystery, intrigue. Many puzzle over the relationship. But everyone pays attention, And attention is something you crave. Taurus can aid you in career matters, but you will have to make some concessions, especially in the financial area.

Leo with Gemini

With Gemini, you are active and inspired. Social contacts improve and there is genuine attraction. Self-improvement programs work both ways here; Gemini tries to improve you, and you try to improve Gemini. The Gemini individual touches that part of your chart related to hopes, wishes, friends—your fantasies are affected by Gemini and could be subject to revision. Gemini is active—associated with Mercury—and this combines with your Leo Sun in a manner that ignites ideas, travel, speculation, plans, reports, and writing.

Much attention is centered on luxury, beauty, or domestic problems when Gemini and Leo get together. The relationship is generally harmonious, despite emotional fireworks. You tend, Leo, to expect too much of Gemini. You expect a sense of humor, charm, versatility—but often, you interpret them as forms of restlessness, dissatisfaction or flightiness. Gemini appeals to you because Gemini flatters you. And, Leo, when you are flattered you find it difficult, if not impossible, to resist.

You admire the quickness of the Gemini mind—you are fascinated by the friends you meet through Gemini. In turn, Gemini is apt to meet his or her match in you where travel, ideas, and general rebelliousness are concerned.

To put it succinctly—Gemini and Leo are *a match for each other.* Whether they are a *good match* depends, of course, on background, environment and the more sophisticated points in each horoscope. But, overall, the combination is favorable—Leo loves bright lights, flattery, and excitement, and Gemini provides these in abundance.

Listen, Leo—you can gain pleasure through this relationship and it could be a lasting one. Don't give it up without much thought, consideration, and projection into future possibilities. There could come a time when you berate yourself for not having accepted what Gemini had to offer.

Leo with Cancer

In relation to Cancer, you are attracted due to an air of mystery—and because you associate Cancer persons with glamour, physical attractiveness, and the good life, such as fine food, drink and cultural attainment.

With Cancer, you strive for material goods, for power, for security. This is because Cancerians touch that part of your Solar horoscope connected with uncertainty, mystery, puzzles—and, in so doing, cause you to go after solutions, to be aware of a need to save for a time when money might not be so easily forthcoming.

There is basic attraction here. The Cancer Moon and your Sun represent symbols of attracting opposites—male and female, hot and cold, fire and water, want and plenty. You have, to put it briefly, *an appetite for each other.*

With Cancer, you become concerned with groups, clubs, institutions and restrictions. There also is an element of the clandestine where you are concerned here. There are expenditures which you consider of a private nature—you don't want necessarily to reveal them.

The Cancer person mystifies you. You see in this individual many persons—mother, lover, cook and provider. Cancer hits that part of your chart concerned with secret fears, phobias, duties.

Listen, Leo: you love mystery, intrigue. Cancer provides it. And if Cancer is smart, you'll hang around a long time trying to figure things out. You need this person in your life at least part, if not all, of the time.

You become more versatile with Cancer. You flex your muscles, and you move toward accomplishment. This relationship is especially good for any association with motion pictures or television.

Leo with Leo

With another Leo, it is a question of who is going to give up the spotlight. Two individuals born under Leo, when together, represent charm, entertainment and personality plus. But it could be too much of a good thing. To make the relationship succeed, each Leo must be willing to step back, to permit the other to show off special talents and abilities.

The Leo man doesn't attract the usual, the mundane, the ordinary. And to succeed in a relationship with Leo, you have to be somewhat eccentric, willing to forgo numerous conventions—and you have to dress well, appreciate good food and be heavy on the compliments. This man is romantic—and somewhat egotistical. But much of the time he's worth an extra effort. No matter how exasperating he may be, he has a right to his ego because he is likely also to be proud of you.

That's a key; make him proud of you. Read, keep up with current events and maintain a sense of humor. He loves to see you laugh, as long as you are laughing *with* and not *at* him. The Leo man demands attention. He is fiery, romantic. He can be an easy victim of the green-eyed monster, too. Very jealous, offended, aloof—if he feels you regard him as anything less than the center of your universe. It's not easy. It's quite a job, handling the Leo man!

The Leo man likes the theater but dislikes theatrics. The Leo male admires beauty but not the "obvious" kind; he prefers the subtle. He is repelled by women who use too much makeup, by women who cry openly (it's much more effective to utilize a dramatic sob), by women who laugh too loud (better to squeeze his hand and smile in appreciation)—and, most important, by women who steal the spotlight. He believes in equal rights for men and women, but expects you to accept the concept that he is just a little superior. He's affectionate and lovable—and he can be yours if you utilize loads of flattery and bat your eyelashes when he turns those magnetic eyes on you.

If you are pursuing a Leo woman, compliment her—tell her she's beautiful and she will be. She has a flair for the dramatic. Let her have the spotlight: but also realize you will have to be unusual—so don't tell all you know.

Maintain an air of mystery. She loves to hear about herself: read her palm and check her horoscope. She demands that you be aware of her. A touch, a gesture, a secret signal—something special—that's the way to woo and win the Leo lady. Your own manner should be regal. She wants to be with someone who is admired by others. In more intimate moments, she admires tenderness, a caress; this is what she prefers to any heavy-handed overtures.

She is sexy but she wants you to want her for more than physical reasons. She values herself. She doesn't give herself away. That is, you must court her; thoughtful gifts mean more to her than the expensive variety. Plainly, romance is part of her life. She is romantic and needs to be needed. She is likely to be attractive, and she expects to be jealous of you, but doesn't want to be reprimanded for her own flirtatiousness. Make yourself a fascinating challenge. Involvement with a Leo woman can be fatiguing, but you will learn about life and living—and love. Her nature is fiery; she is passionate, giving and generous. If you win her, the prize will be a great one. She is stubborn, but she is usually trying to work out what is best for you. Recognize her good qualities, which are numerous. In being amorous, avoid being coarse. Sex, for the Leo lady, is just one part of love. It is the rhythm of life—but to be a part of her life you must first earn her admiration.

She abhors the humdrum, routine, and stupid. She revels in the creative, in excitement, could be an addict of the theater—and she will share the spotlight if she feels you really have something others would admire. She's unusual, complicated, opinionated—but she can be one of the most beautiful experiences in your life.

Leo with Virgo

In connection with Virgo, there is a feeling that money is involved. Listen, Leo: Virgo persons affect your finances. They try to help you but often you resent the aid—and go on a spending binge.

Virgo touches that part of your chart directly associated with money, possessions, and valuables. Virgo makes you aware of domestic and financial responsibilities. There is harmony and a degree of attraction—but it is like taking strong drink or very sweet sweets; you want more, and you press, and Virgo presses—and, if you're not careful, there is an explosion, a separation. That's Leo and Virgo. The Leo Sun and the Virgo Mercury combine to shine with ideas and plans, and the danger always being that the light will become so bright it will burn out.

With Virgo, you become aware of your bank account—or lack of it. Virgo has ideas, prods, criticizes—at times the criticism is constructive if only you will pay heed. Listen, Leo: where you tend to be flamboyant, Virgo tends to be conservative. Where you tend to leap first and think later, Virgo tends to analyze, to draw deductions before jumping to any conclusions. As a combination, the two signs are basically neutral, but can be favorable if you are willing to conserve to conserve health and money.

In all, the association is full of sparks, and one that could ignite into a permanent relationship.

Virgo makes you aware of what money can buy. You become more sensitive to budget. You cut down on some extravagances. Virgo is diet-conscious. You become more concerned with your general health. Virgo is intrigued by you, but frustrated when you ignore common sense in eating, and drinking. You can become impatient with Virgo. But if you select the best that Virgo offers, there are definite benefits.

Leo with Libra

With Libra, you may be confused, but you are stimulated. And for you, Leo, stimulation is the spice of life. It makes the wheels go round and gets the creative juices flowing. That, Leo, is what Libra can do for you.

There could be a lack of solidity in this relationship. We know that we are dealing with Sun signs, and that a complete horoscope takes more, much more than the Sun position into consideration. But, basically, the Solar horoscope does tell a great deal. For example, it tells us that Leo and Libra are compatible—but that you, Leo, tend to deceive yourself in this relationship. You scatter your forces. You run hither and yon. You thrive on the excitement, the beauty, the romance; it is Leo being in love with love all over again. What I am saying is that you must strive for a more practical approach if this relationship is to turn into something of lasting value.

Libra touches that part of your chart related to journeys, ideas, neighbors, hobbies, mental pursuits . . . the ability to take apparently unrelated facts and blend them into a story. Bright conversation is a feature of any Leo-Libra association. It's very pleasant for much of the time—but, Leo, sometimes the edge becomes sharp; perhaps even cutting.

Basically, the stimulation of such an association is favorable. You have great sympathy for Libra. And, Leo, you revere intelligence. This being the case, the right kind of Libran certainly could be the right person for you.

Your Sun and the Libra Venus do add up to romance. However, there are doubts which plague you—and your tendency to be jealous comes to the fore here. You have to work to succeed in this relationship. It could be perfect, if you are flexible. Libra is sensitive and you can be domineering. The answer is to loosen the reins. Libra can teach you much in the realm of art and justice. The question is, "just how much are you willing to learn?"

Leo with Scorpio

There are obstacles here. You want freedom. With Scorpio, there are additional duties, responsibilities. The Pluto of Scorpio, combined with your Sun significator, adds up to sexual attraction. But there is also controversy, because Scorpio affects the part of your chart that is related to domesticity, long-range programs, restriction and parental authority. You display a tendency to rebel with Scorpio.

Some perfectly marvelous arguments could take place here. On the constructive side, disputes clear the air. On the negative level, emotional scars result.

Scorpio helps you with real estate. Scorpio can aid in making purchases of lasting value. With Scorpio, you are forced to be practical. Scorpio could manage your funds. Scorpio could get you to work on time. Scorpio could curb your extravagance. However, in so doing, Scorpio might also curb your zest for living. It depends, of course, on the individual Scorpio and the specific Leo. A complete horoscope comparison is advisable. Generally, the classic Scorpio and the typical Leo have a job to do in making this relationship a success.

You could feet tied down, forced, restricted. But, in the best sense, this discipline could work to advantage. You could be forced to utilize creative talents in a practical manner. Your magnanimous nature would not be wasted on fair-weather friends. You would do more entertaining at home. You would save money. And, with Scorpio, you could put money in the bank and purchase property which increases in value.

Scorpio elevates your standing and aids your career potential. You may rebel, but you also *respond.* Response, for a Leo, is essential. Which means you seldom are indifferent with Scorpio. With all the problems, the ultimate challenge could be worthwhile and lead to success.

Leo with Sagittarius

Physical attraction is featured. The Jupiter of Sagittarius and your Sun blend to provide stimulation. Sagittarius affects that part of your Solar horoscope related to sex, children, creativity, speculation, and general excitement.

With Sagittarius, you seldom are satisfied with the status quo; you want changes and variety. Jupiter and the Sun create an air of optimism. You can expand your interests and find an outlet for some of your hidden talents.

Sagittarius challenges, stimulates, and inspires. You could bring forth abilities that were obscured. With Sagittarius, you could be happy because you are kept creatively active.

Children often add to the happiness of a Sagittarius-Leo relationship. For you, Sagittarius represents adventure; it is the adventure of variety and travel and not knowing what might occur next. The unexpected could become a way of life—and a sure way of retaining youth.

The Jupiter of Sagittarius helps you overcome any tendency toward depression. There is a willingness here to buck the odds, to overcome obstacles, to do what appears impossible. It is always necessary to build on a solid base and, with Sagittarius, this can be accomplished.

There are obstacles. One of the disagreements that could arise is based on where to live, where to settle, what to do in later years. But, the assets outweigh any deficits. Eventually, Leo and Sagittarius could resolve conflicts concerning residence, long-range plans and goals. In the meantime, fun can be had by all.

If you want someone who unlocks the door to your creativity, you have found the right person in Sagittarius. These are two Fire signs; the light could burn bright and result in happiness and achievement.

Leo with Capricorn

Some restriction is evident; the Saturn of Capricorn and your Sun spell responsibility, long-range plans (often interrupted) and some financial pressure. Capricorn affects that part of your Solar horoscope associated with health, employment. With Capricorn, basics are involved, including basic chores and basic misunderstandings.

Leo and Capricorn attract each other; but there is an "edginess" to the relationship. It could get bogged down with details and you might feel held back, restricted. With Capricorn, you could create something of lasting value. Capricorn helps get your name to the right people. Capricorn aids you in sustaining your efforts. Capricorn can discipline you, but it is ultimately for your own good. You don't always appreciate Capricorn, but it might be a case of too much familiarity. Capricorn is reserved and you can be flamboyant. Capricorn takes this in stride, while you would prefer surprise, applause, gasps of appreciation.

Capricorn helps you mature. What Capricorn does, in the main, is to make you aware of some shortcomings. Unless you are mature, you don't take this in stride.

However, if you're mature, this can prove beneficial. Capricorn is patient while you are impulsive. Obviously, Capricorn and Leo can learn from each other, although the lessons are not always pleasant.

Capricorn helps you face reality, which can be a task. You will discover what is of value, what is mere fluff. You may miss the sensational with Capricorn, but you will get the basics. And Capricorn will help you distinguish true friends from those who merely have their hands out.

It's not always easy, but the relationship works if both work at it.

Leo with Aquarius

Aquarius stimulates you; you are attracted, but much in the manner that opposites attract each other. The Uranus of Aquarius, combined with your Sun significator, spells change, travel, variety, communication and challenge Aquarius affects that part of your Solar horoscope related to marriage, partnership, legal affairs, public relations. Your individuality is sparked; you could be angered into action. You are intrigued. You are drawn, but often against your will. Aquarius causes you to examine your conscience, to become concerned with altruistic causes.

You could marry an Aquarius. You could also, on the other hand, become a dedicated rival. Your feelings, obviously, are ambivalent. That's the way Aquarius affects you: up and down, approval and disapproval, elation and anger. With Aquarius, you do not think the same, remain the same as before; you move, change, analyze, get involved.

You are a natural showman. You want attention. Aquarius has interests which are unusual, to say the least;

you are drawn to and want to learn from Aquarius. *But envy exists.* When you recognize this in yourself, you become resentful. Because Aquarius has caused this self-recognition of a weakness, you tend to lash out and blame, accuse. It's a delicate relationship, not always easy. But if it can be made to work, it works well.

Uranus and the Sun—Aquarius and Leo—add up to excitement, discovery, invention, advancement and can lead to a breakthrough in unorthodox areas. Certainly, Leo, this kind of association will provide challenge. Maintain your balance; don't paint yourself into a comer. If you know where you are headed, even though the route is subject to change, this can work to your advantage.

Leo with Pisces

You strive to fathom the "mystery" of Pisces; that sign's Neptune combines with your Sun significator to create pressure, hidden desire, some restriction and a feeling that steam is building toward an emotional explosion.

Pisces affects that area of your chart dealing with the hidden, the occult, with other people's money, with sex and secret information. Pisces is of the Water element; your zodiacal element is Fire. The two do not mix. This means that there are obvious problems—but there is also intrigue which builds into magnetic attraction. Pisces does fascinate you; you want to impress, to show that you are not only worthy, but desirable.

Pisces exhibits a tendency to serve you, to placate, to anticipate your desires and moods. You want the relationship to continue—but in some instances there is a triangle. A third person could stand in the way.

Listen: you take on responsibility when you take on Pisces. There are financial procedures or legal issues to consider. Someone else's money is involved. Pisces represents that part of your Solar horoscope related to the finances of a mate or partner. You could find that funds are tied up in connection with this association.

Be sure, Leo, that you know what it is you *really* desire. Playing games in this area is inviting fire and flood. However, if you're mature and sincere, there could be benefits, both financial and emotional. It depends, of course, on the complete horoscopes of the individual Pisces and Leo involved.

The Neptune of Pisces is compelling where you are concerned; it stands for mystery, illusion and romance—right up your alley!

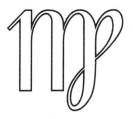

Virgo

August 23 - September 22

Love is serious as far as you are concerned; love is nothing you take for granted. You constantly strive for it, and when you get it you don't let go without a fight.

Where sex and love enter the picture, you think and analyze. You are not of the leave-it-to-chance school. Your sign, Virgo, is associated with Mercury and that is the planet of thought processes. It applies also to this area of sex and love. While many think of sex in a purely physical sense, you tie up sex with the mind, with thought, imagination, ideas and ideals.

When you are in love, your partner can be considered fortunate, for you respond to every nuance of love. You are intent not only on gaining pleasure, but also on providing it. Your average of success in this area can be considered high.

Let me be as frank as possible. Your Fifth House, that area of your chart directly related to sex, is Capricorn, associated with Saturn. This combines with your Mercury to present a complicated picture. And that, Virgo, is one of your main problems where sex is concerned. You make it too complicated!

You are, in your sex attitudes, quite demanding. It is not that you *demand* perfection, you merely *desire* it! Your sexual pattern is one which sees you constantly fighting a tendency to be overly critical. Your greatest adversary, where sexual fulfillment is concerned, is *tension*. Instead of an attitude of acceptance, you reject. Instead of celebrating pleasure, you tend to be critical of release. You worry when you should be gaining and giving; you emphasize responsibility and potential when you should be living for the moment—*the moment*. These, naturally, are negative aspects of your love pattern.

On the positive side, your senses are sharp; you respond to touch, to smells, to sounds, to suggestions. It's necessary for you to draw a line of balance between being critical and being responsive: if you can do so, you will be on the road to great happiness in this area. Your response quotient is excellent, but so is your critical faculty. It is not that you evaluate partners in the physical sense, not in a cool, calculating manner. It *is* that you evaluate in mental compatibility sense: and without this (Mercury), the physical falls apart. Your critical faculty takes over completely from your response. To put it plainly, if you lack mental compatibility with someone, you also will lack fulfillment (love). When thoroughly aware of this, you aid yourself in overcoming disappointment, and heartbreak. If an individual leaves you cold in the intelligence area, the same is apt to be true on a physical level. If an individual is sensitive in your eyes, knowing, *kind,* there is more of a chance on all levels in the area of love. That, basically, is the way it is with you, Virgo.

Your sign is one of the most challenging—and fascinating. You prefer to serve rather than to be served. You teach, you share—you want the finest, the areas of life experience which others merely dream of obtaining. To you, satisfaction and joy are not merely illusions. They are *goals.*

How to reach those goals? Astrology teaches that you first must be satisfied in a mental sense. You analyze, perceive, look to the future as well as reviewing the past. Your standards are high. Some claim they are sky-high.

However, you always are sympathetic, even if critical. You are concerned with pleasing, building the ego of your partner. One of your greatest joys is in giving joy. This applies especially in the sex and love area. However, when disappointed, when the bubble of *mental admiration* is broken, so is the chain of your response level. Then, Virgo, love is like a wild bird: it flies away.

As stated, you respond to a touch, a glance, a gesture: you need to be moved. Often, illusion replaces reality. This is because the Seventh Sector of your Solar chart is Pisces, associated with Neptune, the planet of illusion. The Seventh House represents the outside world—how it looks to you and how it looks back at you. It is also that section of the chart denoting unions, legal ties—in short, marriage. The Fifth House is romance (for you, Saturn Capricorn). The Seventh House is a legal one (for you, Neptune-Pisces). The symbols pile up, become available for examination. They tell us, Virgo, that your hopes, wishes, and ideals are aimed at accepting and being accepted. You *worry* about affairs of the heart. You are pleased, on the other hand, with marriage or the legal acceptance of a romance. Which provides this clue: you would rather suffer in marriage than experience pleasure outside the legal area.

Do you wonder, now, why you often are confused and complicated? Your symptoms, incidentally, are not unique in our society. You seem to have a built-in sense of guilt about pleasure which is not condoned by legal action. Think about this—your Mercury ruling planet tells us you gain understanding through the mental process. Think! Analyze the implications of what has been stated. Such honest analysis could lead to a greater area of fulfillment.

Once you understand, you conquer uncertainty and thus unhappiness. Once you know why you think or respond the way you do, you will react in a manner more desirable for reaching the goal of happiness. In a very real sense, then, astrology can help you along the road to a better and healthier love life.

You are attracted to older persons. You desire an individual with experience. You tend to doubt, even to fear the unknown. You constantly require reassurance. You freeze at uncertainty. This being so, Virgo, it is necessary for you to be knowledgeable in this area. It is a mistake to be squeamish about love and sex. Stop shying away from one of nature's greatest forces—and *gifts*.

Please don't think we are implying here that every person born under your zodiacal sign is exactly the same. But we are stating that the astrological symbols are valid, provide valuable keys, and that you are *enough like other Virgos* to gain insight from this delineation.

Being a Virgo, you want to analyze, deduce, form conclusions, and make changes in theories. You often get so theoretical you forget about the actual, immediate joy to be gained through a mature, fulfilling sexual experience.

In matters of the heart (love), you are often crushed. You win love only to nibble at it until frustration and unhappiness become twin signatures of a relationship. At times, you simply defeat your own purpose. Knowing this, you can now analyze and take steps to enlarge your views, to gain pleasure instead of creating frustration.

Listen: you possess much pride. You insist on quality. But what you are searching for is not always something you can articulate—not without much difficulty. When you find what you are looking for you are not always aware of it. This applies to love as well as to other areas.

You seem intent on fighting yourself. You seem determined not to make life easy for yourself. What are you going to do about it? I would like the answer to be along these lines: "I intend to stop analyzing my pleasure principles to death. I intend to live. I intend to be mature rather than juvenile where love is concerned. I intend to fulfill my potential as a human being!" If you do this, Virgo, your life will change from gray to a rosy-red, from bleak to bright. Take a chance on your instincts. Reject apprehension. Insist on joy rather than criticism. And stop feeling the grass may be greener elsewhere!

Man or woman, you are exuberant, hungry for happiness. You can attain it in love—once you stop being so concerned with security. Now, Virgo, it is not wrong to want a reliable partner, but it often appears you want not only reliability, but insurance—something not always possible in this area. No one can "insure" the future. That is a fascinating part of it: we all are going to spend the rest of our lives in the future. *And it is subject to change.*

Being aware of this, love openly, freely; give of yourself without being too concerned about bank accounts, standing in the community, Dun and Bradstreet ratings. Rich today can be otherwise tomorrow. Poor today can be affluent tomorrow. But one thing that is not subject to change is true love.

Don't trade yourself for an illusion of security. That, after all is said and done, is what it is. But love, despite belief to the contrary, is not illusion: it is, perhaps, the one solid, real thing, the purpose of our very being. If you find love, don't mingle it with apprehension about money.

This is not to say, Virgo, that you should be foolish. I know that you are not a silly person. The point is that you do know the value of love, and you do value it. But if you allow yourself to feel insecure, you become insecure. Then you have difficulty sleeping. Then you no longer can reciprocate. Then you worry love away.

You are discriminating and this is fine—but it is the area of discrimination that counts. Be discriminating in aiding your partner, in building confidence. Then you will be building a solid foundation for love.

Perhaps I am not being articulate. It is certainly no easy task to get across this major point. I would not address myself in this manner to other than a classic Virgo. Plainly, you overthrow your purpose when an aura of uncertainty is created. Once you find love on mental-physical levels, don't find something with which to clutter fulfillment. Love, for you, can be a delicate balance; you can tip the scales in your own favor, or against. Your favor is pleasure, enjoying what you possess, working to better conditions. When you work against yourself, you are nagging. You are berating. You are questioning to the point of raising doubt and sapping confidence. When you do this, you can say good-bye to love. You are sending it away.

Realize, Virgo, that chronological age is no guarantee of wisdom. Choosing age over youth is not necessarily good, or bad: it is the individual who is of major importance. Realize, too, that the future contains one certainty: *change.* If you have faith in your partner—if you do not permit it to be shaken—you do as much as is possible to guarantee change for the better. Otherwise, you surely will be accomplishing the opposite.

In marriage, you are dutiful—and much more affectionate than might be readily apparent to outsiders. In most emotional liaisons, you are proud. But when and if that pride is wounded, you will find the touch of your partner distasteful.

You are neat, tidy—which is fine until carried to extremes. You desire beautiful possessions—which is fine until you break the back of a budget.

You should learn to praise your partner. The more lavish with your praise, the more response is forthcoming from the object of your affections.

You feel that you do know best. Perhaps you do. But carried to extremes, you can create a feeling of impotence in your partner. Obviously, you must utilize your powers of analysis in a constructive manner. This means realizing that you must please in order to be pleased. You cannot constantly criticize without paying a price.

You are unusual, perceptive, and you are capable of creating strength in your partner. You can love with all your heart. And when you do, you find that life can indeed be beautiful. A major key is to avoid depression. If you are happy, so is your partner. If your partner is happy, so are you. This can be termed a circle of contentment: and you must initiate it.

Basically, you hold your future in your own hands. The future is what you make it—and this applies specifically to you. Sex and love can be joyous, fulfilling areas for you—or they can be otherwise. The choice, Virgo, is your own.

How You Relate to the Other Signs

You are physically attracted to Capricorn persons and mentally stimulated by Scorpio. Virgo is harmonious in relation to Cancer, Scorpio, Taurus and Capricorn. Your sign is attracted to Pisces, but many of your qualities and characteristics are in opposition. You're not harmonious with Sagittarius or Gemini. You're neutral in relation to Leo, Libra, Aquarius and Aries.

Of course, this is only a brief view of how you relate to the other signs. There are further details, nuances, and indications. Let's elaborate on some of the highlights.

Virgo with Aries

Oddly, you are apt to fear Aries. At least, you may be slightly afraid of the typical Aries—because you think he, or she, may be taking something which belongs to you, including innermost secrets.

The Mars of Aries and your Mercury combine to whirl your mind, to step up your mental activities. The key is to overcoming this fear is to learn to mauntain control. With Aries, your thinking processes are stimulated. But, unless controlled, you can go off the deep end.

Aries affects the area of your chart that is related to the hidden, the occult, to legacies, inheritance: Aries stimulates you desire for mystery. There are ideas and there is travel connected in your association with Aries.

Money enters the picture and you discuss investments. A broker who advises you regarding long-range investments might be an Aries. Natives of this sign excite and intrigue you, but keep you so active you could become tired with them. Nevertheless, if you need to raise funds, Aries could line up investors.

Aries provides some of the spice of life, some of the mystery, and is instrumental in getting you on a sounder financial footing. With Aries there is attraction, but also resentment from you. You argue; there is conflict, and some of the disagreement could center around who owns what—who is entitled to specific funds.

The relationship is exciting, but you would find Aries headstrong, in opposition to your tendency to analyze before acting. Perhaps a bit of Aries in your life is needed. It depends, of course, on the degree of maturity in both signs, and a careful comparison of complete both of your natal horoscopes.

The combination of Mars (Aries) and Mercury (Virgo) could mean too much, too soon—it's quick, impulsive, exciting, but not without an element of danger. That's the way Virgo adds up with Aries.

Virgo with Taurus

With Taurus the emphasis is likely to be on travel and publishing, on developing a more definite philosophy. Definite attraction exists here; the Venus of Taurus harmonizes with your Mercury. Taurus affects that part of your Solar horoscope that is related to long journeys, the higher mind, publishing and the expressing of your personal philosophy.

Taurus aids you in settling down to a goal, a purpose. That is, settling down in the mental area. Where travel is concerned, you are apt to do plenty of it in connection with Taurus.

Taurus can be stubborn; you are more flexible and it will be up to you to initiate action. With Taurus, your intuitive intellect comes into play. Your powers of perception are heightened. *You find a cause.*

Basically, the signs—Virgo and Taurus—are in harmony. In some areas there are difficulties, which is true of almost all individuals. In this specific instance, the difficulty arises when you want to move and Taurus wants to remain. If too receptive, you could find yourself in a rut, emotional and otherwise. If too aggressive, you could spark a flame of resentment which disintegrates the relationship. You must tread lightly and must always be diplomatic. Remember, you *win* your way with Taurus—you do not force.

Taurus aids you in determining where to go, when and why. But Taurus, left unchecked, could discourage you from going anywhere. What holds you together is that you have much in common. Both signs are of the Earth element and the essentials of life are important to Taurus and Virgo. What could separate you is a conflict of interest in the areas of travel and political opinion.

Taurus can brood, can remain silent and sulk. You are active, energetic and willing to let bygones be bygones. Compromise on the part of both Taurus and Virgo is necessary. The relationship could thrive, and it certainly could prove worth the effort—for both you and Taurus.

Virgo with Gemini

There's a very active relationship where Virgo and Gemini are concerned; the double effect of Mercury (which rules both signs) makes for extreme restlessness. Both you and Gemini might want to lead the way—and so, the relationship is not devoid of some intense arguments. It's very good for business projects but dissension is apparent on the emotional level.

Gemini affects that part of your chart related to ambition, prestige, general standing in the community. Gemini can help you in your career; you make numerous contacts with Gemini, and engage in numerous activities. With Gemini, a desire to get ahead is prevalent. There is no halfway: it's all the way or bust. Much conflict can be avoided if, early in the relationship, the decision is made about who is to give the orders.

Gemini helps sharpen your sense of originality and independence. Gemini accents your desire for admiration. Gemini can get almost anything from you by pretending it was your idea in the first place.

Gemini could be good for your career. Ideas flow at a fast pace. But, Virgo, you will have to be selective. Otherwise, there simply are too many irons in the fire. This means you get involved in numerous schemes, plans, ideas, situations—but this could merely add up to a watering down of efforts, a spreading too thin, a scattering of forces and a basic lack of concentration.

To succeed in association with Gemini, you will have to be a steadying force. Otherwise, arguments ensue and little, or nothing, is actually accomplished.

If you're seeking peace and quiet, Gemini is not for you. If you are seeking to make room at the top for yourself, Gemini can be a valuable ally.

Virgo with Cancer

Cancer activates your hopes and wishes; the Moon of Cancer and your Mercury significator blend to make you moody, and introspective. But Cancer basically encourages you to be a visionary. The signs—Cancer and Virgo—are well aspected.

Your social life improves with Cancer, but you are more difficult to please, harder to satisfy. Your eye is on the future and you tend to want to change your environment.

With Cancer, you begin to enjoy life to a greater extent. Contradiction exists because, with the pleasure, there is also a longing. Cancer introduces you to new friends, concepts. Thus, you are not satisfied with the status quo. You are stimulated—and want improvement, want to make wishes turn to realities. This is not a relationship devoid of problems, but the plus factors appear to outweigh the minus ones.

Cancer is beneficial for you; social activity picks up and you are able to define your desires. It may be upsetting in the sense that you realize what is lacking if desires are to be fulfilled. But you do get at the truth, and this could free you of foolish inhibitions.

With Cancer, the key is to avoid needless brooding. You could, on the negative side, feel alone at a party. Cancer prods you where ideals, career, and income are concerned. Cancer wants security and pushes you to move up, to make contacts, to cultivate worthwhile persons. Your innate sense of humor proves invaluable here; don't permit it to be overshadowed by cynical social contacts.

In all, the Virgo-Cancer relationship is harmonious—especially if you have been in a shell, afraid to really express yourself. However, if you insist on seeking perfection in Cancer, you will probably be inviting disillusionment.

You'll learn some fine points about food, about the good life. And if you can bring forth your wit, your sense of balance and service, then the association could thrive.

Virgo with Leo

Leo mystifies you; with Leo, there is intrigue and the combination of the Leo Sun with your Mercury could blend into an incandescent effect. There is attraction, but the relationship could feature clandestine meetings, secret maneuvers and possibly involve you in scandal.

Leo affects that part of your chart related to secrets, restrictions and illicit romance. Money is involved and the "good life" is lived. You might, as a matter of fact, live it up so much that practical affairs are neglected. Much is hidden in this relationship: you may become enamored of Leo at a time when you are not free to meet openly or be seen together. Somehow, Virgo, the relationship with Leo affects you in this manner: there are deceptions, a third person involved, secrets.

Listen: there is much to favor your association with Leo. Your sense of beauty, and art is enhanced. You learn and can be inspired. You can add to your possessions and you could marry Leo. But, like many other relationships, this one certainly contains its share of complications.

Leo sparks your intellectual curiosity; you want to know the why of Leo. You investigate and you often take the initiative in getting the relationship off the ground. You soon learn how much flattery means to Leo. With your quick, mercurial mind you detect the Leo flaws as well as assets. Leo's romantic nature and highly developed imagination haunt you. You may try to forget, but putting Leo completely out of your mind is no easy assignment.

Leo could help you in television, motion pictures. Leo could aid you in organizing special clubs, and groups. You could succeed in making personal appearances with Leo. The two signs make each other look good.

You could do much worse than Leo. But, despite the good times, an air of apprehension is apt to linger. Keep your guard up; the Leo charm could throw you for a loss as well as delight you.

Virgo with Virgo

With another Virgo, you see many of your own qualities—some favorable, others leaving something to be desired. The relationship meets a main obstacle in the question of who is to be the dominant force. Two Virgo individuals are apt to clash. Each wants to lead, be the critic and work toward a specific goal. But the goal is not always the same. You have much in common, but on the whole, you two may not find it easy to harmonize.

The Virgo woman appreciates money in the bank and wants a ring on her finger. She is discriminating, often regal, and can be tiresome in her pursuit of cleanliness. She doesn't like loose ends; she wants everything to be in place. She wants to know what you're up to; more often than not, she is aware of the details of any project you might be contemplating. She is not easy to fool; it's best to confide in her. If she loses faith in your veracity, you can lose the pleasure of her love. Never, never underestimate her. She knows what it's all about, from business to love. And if you have won her, don't lose her through a patronizing attitude.

The Virgo woman wants to know where she stands. And she wants to stand tall. She must be the highest on your list. Otherwise, you will lose her. She is intelligent, loyal (if you are), frank, discriminating—and she has a wry sense of humor.

The Virgo man is demanding. He doesn't settle for second place. You must make him feel he comes first. He is mercurial, earthy; he usually says what he means—and, most often, he does mean what he says. If you are looking for a slick Romeo, look elsewhere. He is practical enough to be a good provider and sensitive enough to know when you're pretending.

He is practical, honest, fair: he is also basically shy. He has difficulty expressing sentiment. His feelings run deep. But there is an emotional shell. You must be patient and, above all, loyal. If you're considerate, he will rise above adversity and will strive to bring you the gift of happiness. He is the opposite of pretentious. You should aid in building his confidence. He needs a woman who has faith in him, can appreciate his willingness to work toward and achieve major goals. Once he feels he can trust you, he is transformed; he changes from failure to success and devotes his energies toward your welfare.

Virgo with Libra

With Libra, your money sector is affected; you become more discriminating. You select objects of art and beauty, you begin collecting, you start a hobby. The Venus of Libra combines with your Mercury significator to produce romance—but with a definite practicality. With Libra, you do not merely spend, you do so for a purpose: a collection, an investment, the obtaining of a dividend. Where the romantic aspects are concerned, you also tend to be shrewd.

Libra is gentle and you are analytical. The combination could prove of ultimate benefit. And it is a good bet that, if you see it in this light, you will take charge.

With Libra, you set the pace and call the signals, even though Libra may be completely unaware of it. Libra is artistic, just, a seeker of harmony; you can drive a bargain and utilize Libra to help you put across a deal. Through Libra, you can obtain a well-paying situation. Libra can fall in love with you, although it is you who initially makes the pass, takes over, is aggressive, breaks the ice. A Libra who does not have his guard up is putty in your hands.

Your intuition works overtime with Libra; you assume the role of teacher, guiding in health, financial and other matters. An unsuspecting Libra might wind up completely dependent on you.

Though not without complications, the relationship is generally favorable. There are benefits, especially financial. You also can raise your cultural level through association with Libra. You are naturally alert, intelligent, quick; Libra helps smooth some of the rough edges. You're doing all right, Virgo, if you have gentle Libra interested in your welfare!

Virgo with Scorpio

The Pluto of Scorpio, combined with your Mercury significator arouses ambition; and the Scorpio emphasis on your Third Sector causes you to be dissatisfied with things as they are. Scorpio causes you to be restless; with Scorpio there are numerous short journeys, dealings with relatives, a sifting of ideas and a tearing down in order to rebuild.

Scorpio and Virgo are basically harmonious. With Scorpio, you will attract people—along with with their questions and problems.

You succeed with Scorpio in advertising, in a consultant capacity. This is an exciting relationship, but not a restful one. Your forces are scattered; there is an aura of confusion. Ideas are plentiful but lack the basis for personal philosophy. There is much laughter here, but some of it is shrill. Scorpio values you as a friend. You value Scorpio as one who encourages you to wake up and live.

With Scorpio, your ideas are revolutionary. What was accepted is apt to be overthrown. As stated, the signs are well aspected; but the tendency is to drift far afield: original goals are replaced and a general longing to be someplace else takes over.

Disputes with relatives could occur as a result of this relationship. It is an unusual one, to say the least. You become ambitious; you seek greater recognition. Scorpio helps bring people to you. Scorpio spurs you on, makes you desire to spread your views, to break barriers of restriction.

You're going to be active with Scorpio—and that's one thing that's essential where you are concerned. Activity is life for you—and Scorpio can help you to live.

Virgo with Sagittarius

With Sagittarius, there is pressure and added responsibility. But there could also be greater rewards. Sagittarius makes you aware of what must be done and gives you a degree of self-discipline. Rather, Sagittarius causes self-restriction. There is a dependency on Sagittarius—and you strive to learn. But who teaches who is a question likely to remain unanswered.

Sagittarius affects that part of your chart connected with time, home, security, long-range projects. One of your parents could oppose this relationship. It is not without obstacles. For you, Sagittarius could be the voice of authority. The Jupiter of Sagittarius, combined with your Mercury Solar significator, can be exciting. But the plans are grand and the extravagance causes a drain which cannot be plugged.

Listen: you could learn to adore Sagittarius. But the opposition of someone who is important in your life could be like throwing water on a roaring fire. It fizzles.

There is emotional pressure for you where this relationship is concerned. It is anything but problem-free; you tend to attract a Sagittarian who is considerably older than you are. And you learn from Sagittarius, especially about the open road and the open mind. Some of your new concepts conflict with family, duty, tradition. The relationship brings many benefits, but you don't always enjoy them. You tend to feel closed in, restricted—you could feel you are being trapped because, most certainly, the free-wheeling habits of Sagittarius conflict with your own neatness, preciseness. Your pattern is a place for everything, while Sagittarius merely lets things fall into place.

If you desire a greater awareness of responsibility and if you really desire a certain niche, a place in which to build a nest and to settle, Sagittarius is for you. Otherwise, the relationship takes twists and turns which could make you less than happy.

Virgo with Capricorn

You are physically attracted to Capricorn, but the relationship could prove frustrating. The Saturn of Capricorn restricts your quick-moving Mercury; you may find your creative urge is confined.

You are drawn to Capricorn and children could be involved in the relationship. Capricorn affects that part of your Solar horoscope associated with children, sex, speculation, creative resources. With Capricorn, the *desire* is to develop your style; but, at times, the *necessity* is to fulfill duties and obligations. You tend to become impatient. The signs—Virgo and Capricorn—are generally harmonious. Both are of the Earth element and both can be stubborn. You could be overwhelmed by Capricorn. Thus, while the urge is to create, to express, you might find yourself taking a back seat to the needs of Capricorn.

Capricorn causes you to rebel. The rebellion is aimed at standards as they exist, at your personal status quo. With Capricorn, there is change, travel and variety—with the spice of physical attraction an added ingredient. But, basically, the restriction is ever-present, creating a challenge, an obstacle which you feel obliged to overcome.

You pursue creative endeavors with Capricorn. You enjoy what you do . . . for a certain amount of time. Then, Virgo, you decide that you do, after all, know what is best. This creates conflict, especially if the question is related to children.

If you want to release a creative surge, then Capricorn is for you. But if you expect complete freedom, there could be disappointment. Capricorn does not grant that kind of freedom: there are strings attached.

Basically good—that describes Virgo and Capricorn together. And it is very likely there will be at least one Capricorn in your life.

Virgo with Aquarius

You tend to seek perfection with Aquarius: this includes work, health, and security. The Uranus of Aquarius blends with your Mercury significator to stimulate—and also to cause some impractical plans to culminate. What is hoped for is in the realm of the fantastic: the past is to be wiped clean, a new road is to be built, a life is to be lived which is to be devoid of problems: *Shangri-La.*

But life is not a fairy tale and soon there are practical considerations, since Aquarius affects that part of your chart connected with work, health, and relations with associates. Aquarius can be jealous. And you can want to challenge any hold anyone might think he (or she) has on you. Then the idyllic relationship becomes one marred by squabbles, disagreements, sudden flare-ups—even divorce.

In a sense, you feel threatened by Aquarius; you strive to conform. But this striving could be transformed into a break for freedom—with the shadow of Aquarius bearing down. Now, listen: it is not all bad. Much associated with Aquarius is creative, constructive, fun, stimulating. But you are forced to be practical and, unless it's strictly on your own terms, this might not be your cup of tea.

Although Aquarius is no lover of conventions, there is resentment if your mercurial flirtatiousness comes to the surface. You could feel you are being oppressed. Knowing this in advance could forestall difficulty. If you're prepared to forego some desires and activities, Aquarius could be right for you. Otherwise, you might find yourself running away from the relationship.

See Aquarius in a realistic light. Don't build a castle on sand. Life will not be a daydream with Aquarius. It might add up to work, restriction, and responsibility—along with stimulation and advancement. Go into this with your eyes open and you can make a success of the association.

Virgo with Pisces

You are attracted to Pisces, but this could be a case of opposites attracting. Pisces touches that part of your Solar horoscope associated with marriage, partnerships, the public, and public appearances. Forces are apt to be scattered as a result of the combination of the Pisces Neptune and your Mercury. Outlines tend to be hazy. It is a question of not confusing the real thing with fantasy.

Your imagination is stimulated . . . but mostly because you oppose Pisces methods. Which means, Virgo, that you try to find ways and means of asserting yourself. The aspect between Pisces and your sign is an opposition—and, although Pisces tends to play an important role in your life, it is not always a pleasant one.

Pisces makes you aware of your appearance, of the public, of public relations. Pisces is your challenge. Pisces can irritate you because you tend to be precise, while Pisces, in your eyes, can be deceptive.

Pisces and Virgo have much to learn from each other—and often eye each other warily. Basic issues tend to be clouded. And where solid accomplishment is concerned, this combination could be an exercise in futility.

On the positive side, concessions are made, and the two signs learn from each other—perhaps reluctantly so—but nevertheless they do learn.

With Pisces, you don't always know what you want. This tends to cause you to wander, to experiment, to seek greener grass. You could marry Pisces. You could also battle Pisces. And, very likely, you could travel with Pisces.

Long journeys seem to be an integral part of this relationship which, if it gets by early hurdles, might be a lasting one.

Libra

September 23 - October 22

Your love need is a need for understanding. A kind, intelligent, aware person means more to you than one who sparks with personal appeal. The word "togetherness" means more to you than the cliché it has become today. In love, that is what you want—being together. And togetherness means a combining of mental as well as physical forces where you are concerned.

You are affectionate. You are giving. Your Fifth House, which has to do with sex, is Aquarius, associated with the planet Uranus. Combined with your Venus Solar ruler, this depicts some unusual experiences in the area of sex and love. You are physically attracted to Aquarius individuals and also to those born under Leo and Aries. You harmonize with Gemini and Aquarius and, to a lesser extent, with Leo and Sagittarius.

Love, to you, equals responsibility. You take marriage seriously. You are conservative in this area, despite possible outward appearances. The Venus-Uranus combination, to say the least, is unorthodox. Thus, you become involved with persons who are out of the ordinary. All of your experiences are *not* happy ones, but they are exciting.

You are in love with love. You idealize love. You also feel that you have a unique and special ability to mold, to reform the object of your affections. The key, Libra, is to find someone who does not need reforming. You walk into problems and feel you can straighten them out, or, at the very least, extricate yourself. But, as you might be aware from experience, this does not always prove to be the case.

Libra is the natural seventh zodiacal sign, associated with marriage. Thus, marriage is of paramount importance to you, although it could be denied. That is to say that just because the desire is there, the reality does not necessarily follow. There are separations; there is the distinct possibility of more than one marriage. Many Librans, of course, do have successful marriages, perhaps the majority. But there is a constant searching, an idealized version of what love, marriage and a physical relationship should be. In plain words, your personal standards are higher than average. When the ladder is higher, the climb is longer.

You admire—and you require—a partner who does things, who braves the sticks and stones of society, who is extreme, who is inventive, exciting. This is not always the easiest person to hold. There is an abundance of romance in your life. It is better to have loved and lost than not to have loved at all—that sums up your basic philosophy, even though you might not openly admit it.

Some born under your sign, such as Oscar Wilde, defy conventions in this area. Naturally, there is a degree of suffering. Society lashes back; the conventions may frequently be broken, but they are seldom discarded. They come back to haunt.

Listen: you are a beautiful, spiritual person. But you attract many who are not so elevated. You suffer emotional bruises. Love, for you, usually means carrying a burden, accepting added responsibility. Love is not smooth. You have never asked that it be: you only want it to be perfect!

Of course "perfect" is a value judgment. What does it mean to you? It means sympathy, understanding and excitement, plus a community of interests *to be shared.*

Like Leo, you are a sucker for flattery. If you feel someone likes or admires you, it is necessary for you to return the compliment. Now, Libra, this could be fine, provided the person in question is sincere. Otherwise, you are being taken in—in an emotional sense. Why should the world be this way? The answer is simply that it is. Knowing this, if you are a mature Libran, you will be aware. Don't close your mind or heart to experience, but do be *aware.*

You love first on an intellectual plane. The physical response follows—not the other way around. You strive to understand and to be understood. You want to balance, give and take, to receive pleasure but also to provide it.

Uranus, significator of your Fifth House of love and sex, tears away at the usual; it is sudden. You could marry suddenly. Or fall in love quickly. Or out of love just as quickly, suffering emotional scars. You want to experience beauty, especially in your surroundings. You could not be happy with a dullard. When you love, you go all out. You hang on. You strive to comprehend aberrations, eccentric actions: you even make excuses for them. Listen: although you can "fall out of love," you seldom give up hope—that's why you hang on. You seldom, if ever, close the door on romance.

You are capable of deliberately avoiding unpleasant facts, situations. You rationalize. And if your partner is beautiful or handsome, he or she can "get away" with almost anything. That's the way it is with you, Libra. You can deceive yourself where matters of the heart are concerned—and you often wear your heart on your sleeve.

You are charming and attractive to the opposite sex. You are a challenge, and many want to conquer, with you as the victim. Be aware of this and be a shrewd judge. Don't give yourself away to those who are not worthy.

You can be a disappointment to yourself. Being enamored of love, you will, at times, take what is attainable. You will accept what is available. When the quality is below your standards, there is an emotional rebellion. That explains why you can appear to fall in and out of love. But, unlike Gemini, it is really difficult for you to love more than one person at a time. Gemini can do so and get away with it from an emotional standpoint. You don't escape self-recrimination.

You, being associated with Venus, have a deep fondness for luxury. Unlike Taurus, this does not indicate laziness. You are an excellent host or hostess. You will go out of your way to please, to make others happy and to make them feel beautiful and loved. But where details are concerned, you would just as soon leave those to others. Then you are, in your regal manner, ready to take over, to direct, to supervise the serving and the setting.

You know how to dress. Male or female, you make a fine appearance. Your taste is excellent. You are striking, but not gaudy. You can turn on the charm. You can be magnetic. You can draw to you members of the opposite sex. You almost always give the appearance of being someone special, choice. This serves as a challenge. And that is why others resort to flattery, or any other means, to win you. The question is . . . do you want the person doing the "winning?" Realize your hidden powers. Don't charm the wrong person. Some are playing for keeps and you will have to pay the consequences.

Male or female, you are willing to experiment, to bend over to see other points of view. Although you seek the protection of conventions, you are quite willing to shatter them. You have become used to being admired. You are accustomed to praise. You love the spotlight but are gracious enough to give it up to a partner. But you must be sure he or she is worth it. That's the nagging doubt. Where love and sex are concerned, you constantly are haunted by the question, "Should I have done better?" Which is to say you also admire yourself. And you feel you are entitled to the best.

In itself, this is all right. Self-esteem, on the whole, is constructive. But when it becomes a phobia, when you constantly doubt, when you feel that, had you waited, something "better" would have come along, you are asking for trouble. You are not good at hiding feelings, moods. This kind of an attitude could give your partner a definite feeling of inferiority.

You are the opposite of prosaic. You are romantic. You are happy when love rules, when romance dominates. Where pressure in this area comes, then you can become disenchanted. Yet, there is bound to be pressure for you when in love. That's the way it is and the sooner you know it the better for you and your loved one.

You are willing to help a loved one in both a financial and emotional sense. And you usually do. The adventure of mutual effort should be romantic. Make it so. Then romance will be durable instead of fleeting.

One of your negative traits is that you are not above playing one admirer against the other. This is not intended to be harmful, but it often leads to unhappiness. You do this because you feel it is romantic. You enjoy a flirtation. It adds spice. But don't get carried away, especially if you are committed to another. You invite danger because you enjoy excitement, but you could get burned.

Listen: you don't mind if others are jealous of you. But you can't stand it when the situation is reversed. You want to be the apple of the eye; you don't want it the other way around. You want to be sought after, you don't want to do the seeking. In a sense, you resemble Gemini here. But you are more subtle.

You attract those who may not have had your social and educational advantages, no matter what that level might be. You want so much to be looked up to that you are flattered into accepting an inferior product. Is this too harsh? It is true. You know you can do better but, in doing better, would you receive the adulation?

A favorite saying of some Libra women is: "I would rather be an old man's sweetheart than a young man's slave." The key word is *sweetheart.* You, male or female, want to be regarded as a sweetheart, although not necessarily as a "sugar daddy." In fact, Libra men are peculiarly sensitive in this area. They don't want to be "taken," though they often are.

You want to be loved for yourself even though you are not always sure of what that is. The male Libran is frequently a victim of feminine wiles. He loves to be loved, and idealizes that state of affairs. He is eternally young in this sense, no matter how mature in other areas. He would rather be known as a lover than as an intellectual. This he has in common with Leo!

Your sign is the sign of love. Not so much of sex, but of love and admiration and fulfillment. That's on the positive side. On the negative side, your ego takes over and you concentrate on physical aspects to the elimination of other areas.

There is no doubt that you, Libra, are a sensitive lover. You sense the needs, the moods, the subtle nuances of your partner. You are rare. You have been described as a jewel in a world of rough stones. That's a lot to live up to—but you like a healthy challenge.

As a Libra woman, you are apt to be sought after by older men of means: you are such a gracious hostess that such a man seeks you out to impress friends and business associates. If you love such a man, the result is harmony. If love is absent, there could be emotional upheaval.

At times, you attract persons of the opposite sex who are less than sensitive. Then it is you who showers the love and receives a dry bath, which is yet another way of impressing on you, Libra, that life for you without love is no life. Know this and don't deceive yourself into thinking otherwise. More than any other sign, you require consideration, sympathy, an understanding of your needs and desires—and a mental equal. With these requisites present, your days can become songs and your life a symphony.

You often gain financially as the result of marriage. You travel. You add to your wardrobe. Your life changes and becomes worth living. That's why it's necessary for you to be selective. Be receptive, but know what it is you really want and need. Be practical in this manner, even if impractical in other areas.

Love makes a Libran happy. But love, if it is one-sided, can lead to tragedy. Too often, you wear your heart on your sleeve. If the wrong person feels you can be easily swayed, taken advantage of, the die is cast. It's important to assert yourself in a fair but firm manner. If you do this, and if you have chosen wisely, then love is a smile and not a frown.

Try to avoid a marriage of convenience. You do not have to settle for second best.

How You Relate to the Other Signs

Libra is harmonious in relation to Leo, Sagittarius, Gemini and Aquarius. You are attracted to Aries, but much in the manner that opposites attract each other. Libra is not favorably aspected to Cancer or Capricorn and is neutral in relation to Virgo, Scorpio, Pisces, or Taurus.

Of course, this represents the briefest view of how you relate to other signs. There are further details, nuances, and indications. Let's elaborate on some of the highlights.

Libra with Aries

You could marry an Aries; in the case of your Venus and the Aries Mars, there is an abundance of attraction. This involves your basic gentleness and Aries' aggressiveness. It is an instance of opposites attracting each other. Aries affects that part of your chart having to do with marriage, partnerships, legal commitments, public relations, the way you face the world and the way the world looks back at you. The mutual attraction between Libra and Aries is difficult for many to comprehend. But it is there—and it adds up to war or peace, with very little in between.

You want to settle down with Aries; you desire love and peace and harmony. But you could encounter the opposite. You desire balance, but Aries is headstrong and martial. Aries wants to lead and you want to judge. Obviously, the result could be emotional fireworks. This can be exciting—but even so, excitement can wear thin. You know what you want, but you may want more than Aries can provide.

On the negative side of this relationship, you draw upon each other; you sap each other's energy. You come alive but you also become weary, wary and apprehensive. The moments of joy become spaced with times of worry and frustration. With each setback, there are steps forward: you are almost like a general, planning each move.

What starts as spontaneous combustion could conclude in a studied demeanor which is taxing, to say the least.

On the positive side, a genuine attraction can overcome most obstacles. The steps backward become constructive challenges aimed at forward movement. If maturity exists on both sides, marriage, home and family could result.

You learn from Aries; some of the lessons are bitter ones. Others are those you will treasure. I suppose, Libra, one can only say that you will be attracted to Aries, you might join forces with Aries, and it is certainly within the realm of possibility (and more) that you will find happiness with an Aries.

But it won't always be easy!

Libra with Taurus

Taurus individuals intrigue you, mystify you, and, at times, put you in your place.

Both your sign, Libra, and Taurus are associated with the planet Venus—and this is a pleasure-seeking combination. You feel deeply with Taurus. You don't do anything halfway. It is all the way—or nothing. Taurus touches that part of your chart related to money from unusual sources, legacies, a mate or partner's finances, the occult, the hidden, mystery and metaphysics.

Listen, Libra: you are a person who is aware of rights, of justice and injustice. Taurus tends to perch, to protect a piece of ground. In combination, you might become *impatient* with the *patience* of Taurus. Taurus could cause you to borrow money. Taurus affects you in a manner which causes a sigh, a thought that perhaps settling down might be the solution. But to settle down in the comfort to which you both would like to be accustomed takes money. So, a loan—borrowing from partners, friends or a bank—comes into the picture.

The Venus of Taurus and the Venus of Libra spell social activity, luxury. Listen—when you get together with Taurus a dent is made, money is spent . . . loans are negotiated. It could be positive, and could lead to happiness. It all depends on the individual Taurus . . . and on you.

Basically, you will laugh with Taurus. You will enjoy luxury, but you will want finer things, you will need more than mere possessions. This is where Taurus could fall short. You may feel Taurus is too blunt, too earthy. You could say things which hurt Taurus. And once Taurus is aroused, there is retaliation. The relationship succeeds as long as there is laughter. After and beyond that . . . it depends on how the complete horoscopes harmonize, or otherwise. It certainly, however, is worth a try!

Libra with Gemini

Gemini is restless and, where you are concerned, this proves contagious. That is, the restlessness of Gemini "gets to you." And it is quite evident when you are with Gemini: the desire to travel is accented. Also, a relationship with Gemini spurs your creative urge, makes you want to write, publish, advertise. The Mercury of Gemini and your Venus can combine so that you rise above petty details, flaws. But, Libra, it will be up to you to provide the balance.

The two signs—Libra and Gemini—are harmonious, in trine aspect. A friendly relationship exists almost from the beginning. You "hit it off," share similar qualities, even though you are much more sedate than Gemini.

There is an intuitive force that exists when you get together with Gemini. You are inspired to teach, write, develop your personal philosophy. Mercury and Venus blend to bring about appreciation of beauty, to make you better able to evaluate objects of art. You could become active in importing and exporting with the aid of Gemini. You certainly will travel; you begin to know what people think and desire. You are able to anticipate trends, and cycles. You are able, with Gemini, to articulate your thoughts, opinions more effectively.

Obviously, the relationship is favorable. Gemini and Libra are different enough—and enough alike—to keep the spark of interest glowing. Your ideals are stimulated here; your goals are brought into sharp focus. With a Gemini, you can accomplish much, if you don't try to do too much at once. There could also be a tendency to procrastinate. Thus, there are extremes: either an attempt to try everything at once, or a tendency to wait too long. Finding middle ground, a Libra balance, could assure the success of a relationship with Gemini.

Libra with Cancer

You get down to business with Cancer; the Moon of Cancer and your Venus blend to attract money and responsibility. There are disagreements here; the signs are not well aspected. However, Cancer affects that part of your chart related to career, standing in the community, prestige and important enterprises. Cancer may be too practical for your taste, but there are some common bonds which could hold you together.

Cancer could teach you the value of money. Cancer could stimulate your career. And Cancer definitely stimulates your appetite for success. Your ambitions are awakened in association with Cancer. Natives of this sign have a knack for pushing you to your full capabilities. There is no malingering with Cancer; you do or you don't. And it is very likely you *will*.

After you achieve a basic goal, the relationship could bog down; you might tend to lose interest. Cancer looks up to you, and thinks of the future. But the Cancer view, with you, is apt to be long-range, while you are sighting a more immediate goal

The Moon-Venus combination is romantic, but not necessarily capable of withstanding rough spots. This means, Libra, that you will be attracted to Cancer, even fascinated, but when the initial glow wears off, the question of survival could produce a negative result. The base may not be solid; the cards could come tumbling down. After a goal is achieved, Cancer may want to go on, to save for that proverbial rainy day. You may, on the other hand, want to enjoy your gains, especially along cultural lines. You may want to pursue an artistic course, while Cancer could be ultra-practical, especially where food and money are concerned.

In all, this is an interesting combination and *might* spell a success story. On the emotional level, much depends on how each sign "gives," and how many concessions are made on both sides.

Libra with Leo

Your social life improves with Leo; there is attraction and the signs are compatible. Leo affects that part of your chart having to do with friends, hopes and wishes. With Leo, you are going to get out and around; new friends, revised desires, a more outward view are indicated. Leo sparks your creative urge. The Leo Sun and your Venus combine to make you an envied couple. The relationship is largely built on romance—and illusion. Much of it can be considered beautiful; some of it is wishful thinking.

Neither Leo nor Libra takes kindly to criticism; flaws repel both signs. Both you and Leo will have to be aware of the other's sensitivity.

For you, Leo represents a bright spot, although some of Leo's claims, aspirations and activities could leave you slightly agape. The two signs together—Libra and Leo—tend to become involved in some unbelievable situations. The key is to separate illusion from actuality. With Leo, you tend to see people and situations in a rosy kind of glow; there is danger of self-deception. It's important to know what is real and what is illusion, to transform imagination into a genuine creative force. Otherwise, disillusion sets in and the relationship could suffer. Your innate sense of balance must be called into play.

Leo is showmanship and a bright light; you are gentle and romantic. Together, there is beautiful music. But there are some practical considerations. For example, it probably will fall to your lot to watch the budget. Leo can be extravagant. You enjoy this to a degree, but you must also know when and where to draw the line.

Libra and Leo seek perfection. When practical matters impinge on the relationship, the durability of the combination rests on whether or not there is sufficient maturity.

There is romance, beauty, and adventure here. Perhaps one shouldn't expect or ask for much more!

Libra with Virgo

You will meet secretly, make clandestine agreements and generally find that romance can be delicious. But, Libra, a third party could enter the picture and the specter of the Green-Eyed Monster is ever-present. This is not to say the relationship cannot succeed. The Mercury of Virgo combines well with your Venus; there are fun and games, but that part of your chart associated with secrets, confinement, or doubts is stressed by your association with Virgo. Your sense of fair play could be offended by Virgo, but you simply cannot help being intrigued. Virgo lets you in on secrets you feel you should not hear; Virgo confides information which you might find embarrassing. But, with Virgo, you also are introduced to worthwhile organizations, including charitable causes which appeal to your sense of justice.

Virgo gains in a financial way from this association. You gain in a romantic manner. Together, there could be mutual gain, but there is an aura of secrecy. Virgo does tend to "hide" things from you. To insure success, insist on the facts, not promises. Insist on solid commitments, not vague implications. Virgo is restless; you are idealistic.

Together, there could be an intuitive feeling of how things *might* be. But how they actually *are* may be something entirely different. Libra with Virgo can be successful, but there are also undercurrents of discontent as Virgo experiments, laughs, criticizes and flatters while Libra attempts to balance, beautify and justify. This can be most unusual; don't get involved with Virgo if you're not playing your best game, because this one is likely to be for keeps. The stakes are high, and, if caution is thrown to the winds, scandal could erupt.

Listen, Libra; you are going to gain some insight and you may suffer some embarrassment here. But you will, most certainly, learn where you stand on the ladder of experience. And this could compensate for whatever negative actions result. Libra and Virgo—it could last. But in the long run that must be left to the individual Libra and the Virgo concerned.

Libra with Libra

With another Libra, you share numerous experiences, many of them beautiful. There's lots of laughter, much art and light, but not too much staying power. This relationship is good for fun and games, but where settling down is concerned, there are apt to be problems. You come down from the clouds to face everyday realities and the relationship undergoes a marked change. It can work, but it requires wisdom and maturity.

The Libra woman takes marriage seriously. She takes a relationship seriously. She is not apt to be promiscuous. She wants beauty and considers you a beautiful person. You can easily hurt her. She has character. You will have to be considerate or you will lose her. You will have to be kind or you will disillusion her. If you succeed in winning her, you will have won for yourself an opportunity for peace, contentment and love.

The Libra man is sensitive, so much so that he can make you a nervous wreck. Please him but don't baby him. He wants to be manly. Praise and flatter him, especially along sexual lines. He is considered to be delicate, but he is lusty enough to fulfill your needs if you love him. To keep him, you will have to be aware of your appearance. He notices bulges in the wrong places! He may deny it, but he loves being told how handsome he is, how talented, how loving, how exciting. He's fragile, but worth the trouble.

Libra with Scorpio

Your finances, personal possessions, your desire to acquire—these are affected by Scorpio. The Pluto of Scorpio, with your Venus, has an electric effect. You are, with Scorpio, independent and willing to take a chance; you become a pioneer with the spirit to match. There is great attraction here, but you tend to be slightly selfish. You want to add to your possessions. Scorpio gives you the feeling that gain is not only possible, but likely.

With Scorpio, you become more independent in thought and action—with, also, a tendency toward selfishness. That is, you know what you want and you insist on having it *because it is within reach.* This is not like you. But, with Scorpio, there is a brightness, a hardness, a need—and you will go all out to fulfill it.

Scorpio is fine for you in connection with new projects. If you want to embark on a unique, even a daring mutual project, Scorpio is the one for you. Scorpio can help you raise capital; Scorpio can help you obtain genuine bargains. Scorpio can add to your possessions.

There is physical magnetism here; you are drawn to Scorpios. There is also conflict. You and Scorpio both desire to be first. Usually, you are gracious enough to wait, to demur, but when you're with with Scorpio something gets into you. Impatience becomes the order of the day; it is a quest for being there first, for striving, for staking a claim.

It's an exciting relationship. But who will be the boss? That question should be settled at the outset. It is important where Libra and Scorpio are concerned. And who will do the budget? That, too, is important. Preferably there should be a division: one handles the money, and the other makes final decisions on what to do with it. This is delicate, but necessary with Libra and Scorpio.

Libra with Sagittarius

Your mental faculties are challenged by Sagittarius; there is much activity in connection with short journeys, reports, dealings with relatives and neighbors. With Sagittarius, you put ideas on paper, you form conclusions and policies.

There can be a sense of completion in your relationship with Sagittarius. The two signs are favorably aspected and, if you find yourself in a mental rut, Sagittarius is a very potent antidote.

Sagittarius stresses that part of your chart representing family, reunions, hobbies. Sagittarius encourages you to assert yourself. With Sagittarius, you become a self-starter. You begin putting your ideas into motion.

On the negative side, Sagittarius confuses you. There is a tendency to try too much at one time, to spread yourself thin.

A constructive suggestion is to be sure you finish one thing at a time. Sagittarius means well but tends to view projects as a whole, to talk about dreams instead of getting down to the facts of the matter. You, Libra, prefer balance and a solid foundation. The combination of Libra and Sagittarius can be pleasant, even fruitful.

But both have to give a little—and when you do, it is good for each of you in the end. Realize this—and make the first concession. Then, Libra, you do gain from this association.

The Jupiter of Sagittarius, with your Venus, combines to make dreams come true. A wonderful dream is the keynote of the association. But do realize there is more than Air (Libra) and Fire (Sagittarius); there is also Earth, and there are practical matters.

Give this a try, Libra. It could be beneficial.

Libra with Capricorn

There is discipline and restriction with Capricorn. The Saturn of Capricorn blends with your Venus to symbolize responsibility. Capricorn affects that part of your Solar horoscope associated with age, long-range planning, home and solidity.

With a Capricorn, you might feel confined. There is great emphasis on security. And if it is a home, a solid base, a familiar routine which quells restlessness, then Capricorn is for you. But the two signs are different; not opposite, but different in the sense that where you seek beauty, Capricorn is after prestige, standing, a final place to land. Capricorn could be your anchor. This is a port in the storm, or a mere weight, depending on the individual Capricorn and the individual Libra.

Listen, Libra: Capricorn does not provide a problem-free relationship for you. If you are not willing to settle down and to play for keeps, get out of the game. Saturn makes demands; this means that most of the concessions will be on your part. Know this and make adjustments. But if you can't take the heat, get out of the kitchen.

If you have reached basic security in your personal evolution, you have found the right person in Capricorn (depending, always, on the individual and complete horoscope). If it is further adventure you seek, you're probably not prepared for this relationship.

Capricorn helps you find permanent residence and build for the future. Capricorn aids in creating the proverbial nest egg. Libra and Capricorn are not well-aspected, but nothing that we know of is perfect where human beings enter the picture.

On the positive side, your beautiful Venus and the stern but rewarding Saturn could make a go of it. The question is . . . are you ready?

Libra with Aquarius

You are physically attracted to Aquarius; there is a dynamic element here. Aquarius affects your Fifth Solar house; that part of your chart connected with creativity, children, speculation and romance. The Uranus of Aquarius blends with your Venus to provide excitement, the suddenness of discovery.

Libra and Aquarius are favorably aspected; the chances for success are great. The attraction cannot be denied. There is a desire to be one. The key is that you *like* each other.

Listen, Libra: with Aquarius, there could be romance which ultimately leads to love and children. Emotions run deep. This is not a relationship to be taken lightly.

With Aquarius, you are inventive. You try new things and you try to please. There is greater independence of thought, action; there are pioneering activities. Aquarius aids you in becoming a self-starter. In short, Aquarius can be an inspiration because Aquarius helps you come alive. With Aquarius, there is change, travel and an abundance of variety. Life is spiced, and you emerge from any emotional shell.

But the game is fast-paced, and you must not make yourself too vulnerable. In short, you could be hurt because Aquarius touches you where the heart is, where the emotions are, where you care and where you respond. Give of yourself without throwing yourself away. Be vulnerable to the extent that you give freely in an *exchange.* But do not be vulnerable where you do all of the giving and receive nothing in return. Promises are fine, but something of a more solid nature is required. Know this, Libra, and take a mature view of your relationship with Aquarius.

For mutual creative endeavors—Libra and Aquarius fit like a glove. But for details and routine, the glove may be the wrong size, unless both of you are mature.

Libra with Pisces

Pisces affects the area of your Solar chart connected with health, work, and service. The Neptune of Pisces and your Venus add up to a combination of strength and illusion.

With Pisces, basic issues come to the fore. You could lose patience and want to skip essentials. Pisces is not practical as a rule. However, with you—the Libra-Pisces combination—Pisces accents the need to attend to necessities. Pisces helps you keep at it, refine techniques. Pisces helps you appreciate basic services and comforts.

You admire the poetic side of Pisces, but you are wary about the dreams, the illusions. You should, with Pisces, take one step at a time. Pisces, however, can make you trot and finally run, until goals are achieved. The key is to be ready when you arrive.

Venus and Neptune can be a beautiful combination; in this case, the blend is also practical. Obviously, the Libra-Pisces relationship can be successful. Both are delicate to a degree, both have hidden strengths. Pisces helps you take care of your health; Pisces makes you exercise and diet-conscious. Pisces doesn't do this for many people; You can be someone special to Pisces.

Exciting experiences can result from your relationship with Pisces. There is, however, a basic conflict. It centers around whether to accept the practical or to break bonds to defy conventions. The key, of course, is to learn the rules before breaking them. In plain words, be mature enough to know *exactly* what you're doing.

Generally, Pisces and Libra can help each other. And that, after all, is saying a great deal.

Scorpio

October 23 - November 21

Sex, for you, is related to the delicious privacy of intimate moments with someone you love. You are sexually oriented; your creative drives are strong.

Sex, power and material well-being are perhaps more important to you than to the average individual. You are seldom satisfied with the ordinary. You seek improvement, refinement—you seek to feel life to the fullest extent.

The Fifth Sector of the chart is related to sex. The sign in the Fifth House of your Solar horoscope is Pisces, related to Neptune. This combines with your Pluto significator to create highly charged emotionalism. When you give of yourself, it is all the way. You are willing to tear down barriers in order to build a wall of security. When that wall is threatened, you rear up, you rebel, you prepare to do battle.

You are more than capable of holding your own under pressure. In fact, you can withstand long, continued pressure which would break down the constitutions of most other people.

In a sense, your outlook is creative, or sexual. Sex, for you, is the creative process. Out of nothing, you build. From a secret desire, you nurture a flame of love. From within you comes an outpouring of love. Not all recognize it as such, but when the right person does, your life becomes a song.

You are capable of using powers of personal magnetism. You are attractive to the opposite sex. On the negative side, you tend to take advantage of this quality—you can abuse it and "bully" those less forceful.

On the positive side, you help others to enjoy life, to be forthright, to be creative, to realize their potential.

Listen, Scorpio: you are an individual filled with contradictions. You want to aid the underdog. But you also want to maintain your own standing. You can hate and love yourself all at the same time. You are a puzzle, but also one of the most fascinating and controversial of the zodiacal groups.

As stated, your Fifth House, or the section of your Solar chart related to sex, is Pisces. That sign is ruled by Neptune. Thus, for the sake of symbolic interpretation, we are able to study your planetary significator, Pluto, in relation to Neptune, the indicator of your Fifth House. The combination of Pluto and Neptune indicates that, perhaps because of your conscious or unconscious concentration on sex, you have more concern in this area than most.

Listen: you deceive yourself more than anyone else would ever dream of attempting to deceive you. You have strength, but can lack confidence. You constantly seek to prove yourself. In sexual activity, this could lead to a kind of frenzy. You want approval and admiration; you feel the need to inspire awe. This could take you on a crazy merry-go-round ride. It is not necessary to prove anything. Love and sex can be beautiful, gentle, rewarding: the only proof' to be offered is that of mutual admiration, mutual pleasure, a reciprocation of affection. If you're mature, mentioning these words is not necessary—you are already aware. But, if you're emotionally underdeveloped, these statements are very necessary. You are intense and you want to be loved. If you relax, you will have a greater chance of finding the kind of fulfillment you seek.

Now, let's attempt to get deep inside the real you. The Pluto–Neptune combination tells us you tear down what is you—you try to surround yourself with mystery, and glamour (Neptune). That is to say, you tear down the actuality of your being in an attempt to replace it with something nebulous, something that cannot really be touched. You are, in effect, protecting yourself from emotional involvement. Thus, Scorpio, while you want love, you are reluctant to trust others with your complete being or self. You attempt to create a substitute, saying in effect, this cannot hurt me because it is not me. But, when you become involved in an intimate relationship, substitutes will not do. It must be you, completely involved and vulnerable. The sooner this lesson is driven home, the better.

Your sign is complicated; it is impossible to pigeonhole. You are many things to many people and very confusing, even to yourself. In the sexual area, you react in extremes: you are either cold or hot, giving or demanding, generous or selfish. You want to handle responsibility. You want to call the shots. And this often affects your timing. This is the timing that makes love an art rather than a mere act.

What, then, is to be done to make you want to help yourself and to make your life in this area more satisfying and gratifying?

First, it is necessary for you to relax your grip. You become overly concerned with power, with material possessions. When you become tense and concerned, you chase away love, gratification and ultimate satisfaction.

These indications, while perhaps applicable to many, are intensified where you are concerned. Letting go is essential to your emotional welfare. Relaxing within is the key to greater emotional fulfillment.

You possess intense pride. The intensity of your character dominates almost everything else. You are intense in work and love. This being so, you are also sensitive. Jealousy is no stranger to you. You want to please, to be wanted, needed; you want to leave an impact. You do not want to be regarded as a mere ship passing in the night.

That's not you. What is you is meaningful; your relationships must be important and significant, especially in the love area. There is no halfway here; you need complete attention—and appreciation.

Scorpio, you are concerned with making your mark—so much so that you could not only forget your own pleasure principles, but those of your partner as well. That is why it is so important for you to let go. Give of yourself and let the chips fall where they may—that remains basically the key.

The sign on the cusp of your Seventh or marriage House is Taurus, associated with the planet Venus. This makes you very idealistic where legal union is concerned. And, Scorpio, it makes it almost impossible for you to feel you have achieved the ultimate. That is, you want your mate to reach a height which perhaps only you can reach. This is a fine ideal, but it could place quite a strain on the individual in question.

Now, of course, you do possess many positive qualities in this area. For example, you are vigorous, passionate, giving and concerned with the welfare of those who love you. Often, in fact, you are more concerned with the happiness of others than you are with attaining self-fulfillment. Naturally, a balance must be struck in order for the relationship to create mutual happiness.

Your intuitive qualities enable you to make the people you love happy. You are capable of giving pleasure, more so than when it comes to receiving the same. Again, the key is to let go; loosen your grip. When you love, relax. Otherwise, it might be something other than love.

You possess great curiosity. You are never satisfied simply to know that something happened; you demand to know *why* it occurred. This carries over into the love and sex area. Your desire to please leads to questioning, and much of it is self-query. In turn, this could be transformed into a kind of self-doubt which ultimately could breed frustration.

Your Twelfth Sector significator is Venus, the same planet which holds sway over your marriage sector. Your idealism, thus, cannot be doubted. It is Venusian, which means that you seek love in a true, idealistic sense. But you very often confuse love and sex. Most certainly, sex is part of love, but also it is most certainly not the complete story. For you, love means not only physical compatibility, but also intellectual harmony. This realization could aid you in the important and necessary process of letting go.

Your Fifth House, Pisces, indicates that you are attracted to someone who is mysterious. You want to learn secrets. And if someone you love confides in you, you are gratified. You want to be trusted with confidential information. And the more confidence between you and your partner, the better. You want others to be dependent, to be deadly serious where you are concerned. Anything less is not designed to please you.

For you, man or woman, love is a mystery, sacred, private: you don't want to share someone you love. You are possessive—and, as a matter of fact, proud of it. You are jealous—and, as a matter of fact, pugnacious about it. In the area of sex and love, there is no halfway with you, no playing of games. If you find yourself becoming involved with a flirt, do something about it. Don't ask for punishment. It doesn't pay for you to become involved with someone who is going to cause misery.

You are perceptive, intuitive enough to see through people who say one thing and mean another. Insist on the philosophy that actions do speak louder than words.

Listen: you are capable of overcoming adversity, and of absorbing punishment. Now, every relationship is not going to be perfect. But the point is that you must steer clear of inviting trouble. Which means, Scorpio, do not deliberately become involved with someone who, intentionally or otherwise, is going to hurt you emotionally. Your intuition gives you signals; pay heed to it.

You can marry to your own financial advantage. You can marry to your emotional advantage. You can marry well and be happy. You can do these things if you will.

You are not only intense, you are proud. Because of your pride, you make demands on your mate—to climb higher, to attain greater levels. In a sense, this is constructive. On the negative side, the intensity of your pride creates a problem. An attitude could prevail that there is no pleasing you. Avoid this—be constructive in your criticism. Mix praise with demands. Maintain a balance so that you don't defeat your basic purpose.

You have the capacity for lasting love. But you nurse grudges. You can love and hate; you can be warm and cold. You must never use sex as a weapon. This is a temptation where you are concerned. But if your mate or partner comes to regard you as one who doles out sex in the way someone else might offer food to a trained dog—you are on the way downhill in that relationship.

A business or financial arrangement often enters the picture in connection with a Scorpio marriage. It seems quite natural; not a hard bargain, but an agreement. You are drawn to people who do things. You want a partner who is active, who invests time and talent and money in something you can own and direct, too.

Marriage, for Scorpio, can be heaven or hell. With some of the hints provided in this chapter, it is hoped that your marital adventure will be accompanied by the singing of angels.

You associate love and sex with intimate, quiet moments when the answers come from within. It can be that way, too. It is really all up to you. You can be the master of your own destiny, because character is destiny. Mold your own character and thus create your own destiny.

How You Relate to the Other Signs

Scorpio is physically attracted to Pisces, and intrigued by Libra. You are harmonious in relation to Virgo, Capricorn, Cancer and Pisces. You are attracted to Taurus, but much in the manner that opposites attract each other. Nevertheless, you could marry Taurus. Scorpio is not favorably aspected to Leo or Aquarius and is neutral in relation to Libra, Sagittarius, Aries and Gemini. Of course, this represents the briefest view of how you relate to other zodiacal signs. There are further details, nuances, indications. Let's elaborate on some of the highlights.

Scorpio with Aries

Aries has an odd effect on you. The Mars of Aries and your Pluto can coincide with frustration. Aries is Fire and you are Water; the two do not mix, which is not to say that the relationship cannot succeed. What it does indicate is that there are problems, more so than two individuals might normally expect to encounter.

Aries natives could irritate you. You sympathize with their goals and their desire for independence. In sympathizing, you feel you should do something. But no matter what you do, you feel it is not enough. This creates a guilt feeling, followed by irritation. That's why the relationship could be described as odd.

Aries affects that part of your Solar horoscope related to work, health, the ability to harmonize with co-workers. Aries affects your employment, your ability to rise above your environment. With an Aries, you work—and enjoy it. You perform services. Aries helps you in a steady manner, is not sensational, but reliable.

With Aries, you might feel bogged down, buried in details, surrounded by red tape. You get impatient. You could act impulsively, pushing logic aside.

Both signs possess a keen desire for independence. Both tend to be dominating. Naturally, this could create problems. Diplomacy is essential in any association with Aries. Otherwise, conflict results, followed by animosity and a breakup.

With Aries, you get the job done and have the courage to overcome obstacles. It's not easy, but it can be done. It depends on the individual maturity of Aries and Scorpio. There is attraction. You are drawn to each other. The problems can be overcome. It is worth trying!

Scorpio with Taurus

Taurus is your opposite number and there is profound attraction. You could marry Taurus. The Venus of Taurus and your Pluto combine to inspire independence, originality, a breaking from patterns, unorthodox methods. Taurus affects that part of your chart associated with marriage, legal contracts, public affairs, partnerships and public relations. You are drawn to Taurus much in the manner that opposites attract each other. You can both be stubborn. Neither one is easy to live with—or to live without.

With Taurus, your viewpoint changes. You begin to see life through Taurus' eyes. Taurus helps you appreciate luxury, beauty, the sensuous side of life. Both you and Taurus are passionate beings: a love relationship could be profound and meaningful. A partnership could succeed because you complement each other. But there are disagreements and it would not be wise to leave an argument hanging. This means: settle differences as soon as possible. Trying to bury a grudge doesn't work; it smolders and erupts. You can't force issues with Taurus. You learn to be patient or the relationship does not last.

With Taurus, you embark on new projects and adventures. But you constantly see, feel, hear, sense and react in a Taurus manner. You, thus, could feel dominated. Taurus will not change, at least not without a firm struggle. Both your sign and Taurus are fixed, obstinate, determined; you're each convinced that what is right for the one is right for the other. One of the two is going to have to decide whose will is to be the dominant one—there can only be one captain on this Taurus-Scorpio ship.

If you want to shut out the past and get going with new experiences, you've found the right person in Taurus.

Scorpio with Gemini

You broaden horizons with Gemini. You delve into areas that you previously considered to be restricted or taboo. Your mental resources are brought into play, and your curiosity is sharpened. The Mercury of Gemini blends with your Pluto significator to take you out of yourself. The restlessness of Gemini serves as a challenge.

Your Eighth Solar House is affected, and both you and Gemini are concerned with money, the occult, legacies, and hidden matters. With Gemini, you investigate ways of gaining a greater reward for efforts. Gemini discovers a part of you that very few (perhaps even you) knew existed. Gemini works to enhance your reputation. With Gemini, you have a chance for getting your viewpoint across to a greater segment of the population.

This is a good working relationship, but there are personal problems. You are somewhat frightened by Gemini. Perhaps this is because Gemini reveals so much about you—to you. Gemini analyzes, asks questions, probes deep into your inner self. You feel challenged—and you react. There is attraction on a physical level—but it is likely to be you who are most attracted in this manner.

With Gemini, many concepts of the past are discarded. You look to the future and are more aware of the possible results of your actions. Gemini makes you *aware.* This is not always an easy process—in fact, it can be painful. Many things that you formerly took for granted are reviewed—and some are changed. It's not always easy, but it can be constructive.

You do more listening and learning with Gemini. The relationship is constructive, though not always durable. If you want to make it last, it is necessary to take a long-range view, to overcome petty annoyances and to perceive the many charms of Gemini. If you want to live—and learn—Gemini is for you.

Scorpio with Cancer

You harmonize with Cancer, because the Moon, ruling planet of Cancer, combines with your Pluto to promote a constructive relationship. You could marry a Cancer because there is, with a native of this sign, a desire to settle down and have a home of your own. Cancer affects that part of your chart having to do with long-range planning. You look ahead; you make adjustments. You begin to utilize your assets more intelligently. You begin an investment program. You gain power because more people become aware of what you're about—with Cancer, there is a solidity and you can bring together dissenting factions.

Listen: you possess loads of power, creative ability which needs an outlet. Cancer helps find that outlet. Cancer makes a home or makes it possible for you to obtain a place you can call home. The Moon of Cancer has a magnetic appeal for you. Where disruptive elements exist, they evaporate when you get together with Cancer.

Both Cancer and Scorpio are of the Water element; both are sensitive and predisposed toward being psychic. There is a bond of understanding here. You could meet a Cancerian and feel you have known that person for a number of years. The appeal is on mental, emotional and physical levels.

Now, listen: I am not attempting to describe some sort of utopia. Not all will be perfect with Cancer, nor with the native of any other sign. But the odds for your success with Cancer are greater than with numerous other natives. There is no sensational blast; the evolvement is gradual, but the progress is steady. You build, with Cancer, on a solid foundation.

If patient and perceptive, mature and receptive, you could find greater happiness and fulfillment as a result of your association with Cancer. In actuality, Scorpio, of course, it is up to you.

Scorpio with Leo

Leo helps you investigate opportunities. But Leo is a Fire Sign and this does not mix with your Water element. This means there are problems, but none that cannot be overcome. Leo fires your ambitions. With Leo, there is change, variety, physical attraction and you also are mentally stimulated. At times there are disputes. Both are fixed signs; both ran be stubborn. Both want to lead, to dominate, to provide sage advice. The key is to take turns listening!

Leo affects that part of your Solar horoscope associated with career, ambition, prestige, and standing in the community. You gain greater fame, recognition and power with Leo. Together, you could build an empire!

But how you get on in a strictly personal relationship could be another story, as the two signs are not well aspected. The chief problem appears to be a tendency for one to try to impose his or her will on the other. Leo is strong, so is Scorpio. Leo strikes that area of your chart making you want to express, to rule, to dominate, to advance, to make room at the top. Leo makes you aware of potential, of possibilities, of power. With Leo, you are not going to be satisfied with the status quo; you are going to want to get a business of your own, to write rather than receive directives. With Leo, you will want to dictate the pace and, with Leo, you could successfully begin an enterprise which brings with it opportunity for change and travel and the excitement of discovery.

With Leo, there is physical attraction and ambition. The relationship is not without problems. But many of these are overcome by the intense activity, the adventure of success, the anticipation, the realization that the sky is the limit.

Basically, even if the association is not permanent, you probably would not trade the experiences encountered with Leo.

Scorpio with Virgo

There are good aspects here; Virgo enhances your social life and brings you friendly contacts. Virgo affects that part of your Solar horoscope connected with wishes, desires, friends. The Mercury of Virgo blends with your Pluto to expand contacts, to put solid ground beneath your aspirations. What you do gains a better reception with Virgo on your team.

The emphasis is on appealing to a larger segment of the public. Beautiful dreams can become realities. Virgo has ideas and you have creative force. Together, there can be what amounts to universal appeal.

Listen: this depends on the individual Virgo and the individual Scorpio. At best, there is popularity and profit. At worst, there is extravagance, much promise, but a failure to carry through on unique proposals.

The Virgo-Scorpio combination is a good one. You can complete projects and you can create items that are needed. But patience and persistence are requisites. Virgo can be restless and you can be obstinate. If mature, you can overcome the negative and accent the positive. That will be necessary if success is to crown your mutual efforts.

On a personal level, the attraction is there, but it may not be permanent. You will have to dig deep for true understanding. Virgo is on your side and wants you to succeed. But you will have to return the compliment. Friendship is a two-way street and this is a lesson pushed home by your relationship with Virgo.

The combination of Pluto and Mercury tends to rejuvenate, to put new wrapping on established products. But, basically, this is superficial and additional aid is required. You succeed with Virgo, but you require outside help. Luckily, Virgo can put you in touch with the right person.

In all, excitement and adventure are spelled out when Scorpio and Virgo combine forces.

Scorpio with Libra

Libra is romantic where you are concerned. And, from your point of view, Libra is mysterious. With Libra, you become more creative, more concerned with the theater, with being where cultural events are occurring, with being a part of a creative revolution. The Venus of Libra and your Pluto combine for excitement, discovery, romance, independence, a shaking off of the past.

Libra affects that part of your Solar horoscope related to secret fears, and doubts. Libra pacifies and excites you at one and the same time.

Listen: you differ from Libra. Some of your views, opinions are the exact opposite. But you are fascinated and willing to share, to learn. You could adore Libra. You could shower Libra with gifts in an effort to please. You'll find Libra opening the door to new concepts. And you do not want to lose Libra.

Libra makes you look behind the scenes. Libra causes you to appreciate the subtle. Libra lightens your touch and transforms you into a romantic. Now, Libra is not perfect, nor are you. But together, there is a chemistry in you both which could ignite into a permanent attraction. The combination of Pluto and Venus is an unusual one. It is not easy to fathom. But it is there, standing unique and tempering beauty with strength. The fragility of Libra is given greater substance by Scorpio. The intensity of Scorpio is given a lighter, more humorous and artistic touch by association with Libra.

This is an especially good relationship for you when engaged in the theater, motion pictures or television. Outside of those areas, it is good for club, group, organizational or charitable activities.

Obviously, there is much that is favorable to commend this association.

Scorpio with Scorpio

With another Scorpio, there is apt to be a struggle for power. Both of you want to handle responsibility. You are attracted to each other, but you are possessive of each other and want to run the show. There are problems, but they are not apt to be financial. Together, you can succeed in business but tend to bury the tender part of the relationship—power and money and responsibility abound, but there could be a dearth of laughter. With another Scorpio, you aim toward success in a big way and could succeed in attaining major objectives.

The Scorpio man won't be satisfied with anything less than your best. Also, remember that he usually means what he says. He has a gift of seeing through pretense. He can perceive, delineate, render shrewd analyses in many areas—including you. Don't attempt to reform the Scorpio man. He knows what he wants. If you want to lose him, start correcting his manners and speech. If you want to keep him, try to understand, sympathize and cooperate.

The Scorpio man is physical, yet emotional; he requires love in its poetic sense, yet can be animalistic—brutally frank, brutally honest. He will, without doubt, let you know whether or not he is pleased. And his pleasure is likely to come from you—if you are pleased, so is he. You will have to be patient-and honest. Confide in him. Let him know, in a tactful, mature manner, where he is pleasing you, where he is failing. If you do this, the Scorpio man is happy and will go all out to make you happy. He can be jealous; if you want him, you will have to meet and pass numerous tests. But it could be well worth the trouble.

The Scorpio woman is emotional, affectionate. She is capable of tearing down the past in order to rebuild for the future. She has an air of mystery, could be psychic, and she is a living lie detector. It's best to tell her the truth, no matter what the circumstances. She'll find out, anyway!

The Scorpio woman is dynamic, explosive, and has a temper. But she is also exciting and fiercely loyal. Don't seek a relationship with this woman unless you are strong, willing to make mental-emotional adjustments—and have a genuine respect for members of the opposite sex. She doesn't want to be patronized.

The Scorpio woman wants the facts, wants to know where it's at, wants to know how much money is in the bank and what the future prospects are. She is dynamic and explosive; she can lose her temper one minute and resemble a purring kitten the next. She can lead you a dizzying pace. She is physically attractive; she is hard to let go of—and you could become addicted to her. She can be forceful, dominating; and she also can be stubborn. But above all, she is warm and can make a man so happy that he'll forget that the word "trouble" is even in the dictionary.

Scorpio with Sagittarius

Sagittarius can be lucky for you in money matters. The Jupiter of Sagittarius and your Pluto combine to create a steady force—one that can break through red tape. Sagittarius affects that part of your Solar horoscope related to money, personal possessions and income potential.

With Sagittarius, the basic flaw for you could be an idealized view of people and situations. There is, in other words, a tendency here to fool yourselves. This could lead to more spending than earning. However, if you are forewarned (as we are attempting now to do), the relationship could be profitable. This is because you find ways, with Sagittarius, of perfecting techniques, of creating intrigue, of providing an air of romantic illusion. And of having people pay for the privilege of basking in this aura!

Sagittarius is expansive, philosophical, fond of travel and very expressive. You, Scorpio, can be fixed, secretive. The blend with Sagittarius should be beneficial. New horizons appear; you find an outlet for your intense feelings. In doing so, there is profit—emotional and otherwise. At times, however, you frighten Sagittarius. Your moodiness and possessiveness could send Sagittarius away. Know this, and if the relationship means much to you, open up and be pleasant more consistently. Being consistently pleasant will become a habit, a natural part of yourself. This is not to paint you as an ogre. It is just to say you do tend, very often, to live within yourself. This makes it difficult for others to communicate. You smolder sometimes. When that flame is fanned, it can emit a rush of heat, too hot for many to handle.

Sagittarius is a Fire sign; your element is Water. There are problems because the two do not mix. You will have to work to make this relationship a success.

But, Scorpio, it could be worth it.

Scorpio with Capricorn

There is laughter, activity, and travel when you associate with Capricorn. The Saturn of Capricorn and your Pluto blend to create action in many places at once. The danger is in scattering your forces, trying to do too much, and in being superficial. Capricorn affects that part of your Solar chart concerned with relatives, short journeys and ideas.

With Capricorn, there is excitement and seldom a dull moment. This is odd, because Capricorn is not always a humorist. And you, Scorpio, can be intense. But the chemistry of Scorpio and Capricorn together create laughter, movement, energy. Some close relatives, especially brothers and sisters, may oppose the relationship. But very few things are perfect; the opposition can be overcome because Scorpio and Capricorn are well aspected.

Capricorn helps you to be more versatile and flexible. You are not as set in your ways with this native as you are with some others: there is more maneuverability. Scorpio is powerful and Capricorn is steady, and can be discipline-conscious. Properly harnessed, this combination can spell success. Certainly, there is flash, and inroads are made—but durability could be lacking. With Capricorn, you want to expand. Pluto and Saturn equal steam and there must either be an outlet or an explosion. The excitement of the buildup is present. The key, of course, is to discover the proper outlet. It may not be easy but is likely to be very much worth the effort.

There are reunions, parties and social affairs which dot your relationship with Capricorn. There are visits and trips; there could be writing and communication with those in other places.

The two signs harmonize. There's much going in your favor with Capricorn. Really, Scorpio, it is up to you to make the most of it.

Scorpio with Aquarius

There are conflicts here, but you two can also get a job done. Aquarius affects that part of your Solar chart related to finishing things, security, home, one of your parents and long-range projects. The Pluto of Scorpio combines with the Uranus of Aquarius to produce a deep-seated feeling that security is elusive. Thus, there is a drive for goods, for money, for anything which seems to add to security. That's a basic key to what happens when Scorpio gets together with Aquarius.

The two signs are not favorably aspected. But, with Aquarius, you can get a business going, can build a house, can create an atmosphere which promotes security. There is physical attraction here, despite the numerous disputes which are likely to occur. It is not an "easy" relationship, although there is a genuine *desire* for harmony.

A Pluto–Uranus combination takes you far from the conventional course of events. What occurs here is sudden, dynamic, exciting. Whether it is constructive or otherwise depends on the degree of maturity attained by the individual Aquarian and Scorpion.

Aquarius is likely to look up to you, to regard you as an asset to his or her career or standing in the community. For you, Aquarius represents a solid base, especially where land and real estate are concerned. You can, with Aquarius, determine values, and this does seem to be specifically connected with a home, real estate, land or property. Aquarius would be beneficial for you in these areas.

Both Scorpio and Aquarius are fixed, and can be determined to the point of obstinacy. You find Aquarius exciting, basically because of what you consider "potential." You constantly take a long-range view here. You overlook current inconveniences, even abuses. If you are seeking instant happiness, Aquarius is not for you. If you're willing to wait, then the relationship could prove constructive.

Scorpio with Pisces

Your sign is well aspected to Pisces. Scorpio and Pisces both belong to the Water element. Both are impressionable; some claim that both Pisces and Scorpio possess extrasensory perception.

With Pisces, you are creative and you get a new lease on life. Pisces affects the area of your chart that is related to children, sex, speculation and creative endeavors. The Neptune of Pisces blends with your Pluto to further intuitive knowing. With Pisces, you teach, you perceive and you are able to rise above petty obstacles. Certainly, this combination holds great promise.

There is great attraction here. Pluto and Neptune create a romantic aura and, once Pisces and Scorpio get together, it takes a storm of considerable proportions to separate them.

With Pisces, you succeed in rising to heights of creative intensity. You hurdle the petty; you teach, write, share knowledge and find an outlet for pent-up energies.

With Pisces, you are able to detect trends, to get the feel of the pulse of the public. The aspect between the signs is a trine, which is very favorable. Great joy through children is indicated for you when with Pisces. You also learn to appreciate your own unique talents rather than taking them for granted. Change, travel and variety are keynoted, too, through this relationship.

You may be slightly impractical here; your ordinarily intense emotional nature is accented. The tendency is to act on impulse. With Pisces, you act first and ask questions later. Being aware of this distinct possibility, take steps to prevent it from running along negative lines.

This could be a permanent relationship; it is loaded with emotional dynamite. Knowing this, don't play games with Pisces.

Sagittarius

November 22 - December 21

The Fifth House of your Solar horoscope, representing sex and love, is Aries, related to Mars. This combines with your Jupiter Solar significator to make you extremely popular. The opposite sex views you as active, dynamic, and fun. You have a sense of humor about sex, which is more than can be said for most people.

Your attitude is apt to be ambivalent. It is not always easy for you to be serious about sex and love. Like Gemini, you can apparently love more than one person simultaneously. Conversely, you want to be loved alone; you don't want to be shared. You believe in the double standard, whether you openly admit it or not. You want to be the sole possessor, but you are not adverse to sharing yourself. You can be the perennial youth: some think you may have all but discovered the fountain that purports to dispense youth. You have no desire to grow old and serious where sex and love are concerned.

Your creative drive is strong. You are, as in other areas, idealistic about love. You think of love and sex as joyous experiences, which is a basically healthy view. Being inwardly joyous is not exactly your strong suit in general. But in the area of sex and love, you do feel that dreams can come true and that ideals can be carried out—that here, above all else, you can find yourself.

You are open in this area; you are receptive and you also are vulnerable. You are optimistic, *expecting* to embrace love and happiness. These are great and natural expectations. Without love, your life is hollow. There is no happiness and there is no satisfaction or fulfillment for you without love.

You cannot abide a narrow-minded partner. Your hallmark here is freedom. You are, however, basically conservative; you want love but you are selective. You want to be loved more than anything else. Love and admiration are twin necessities for you. You can be aggressive and protective. You draw to you those perfectly willing to lean, to take advantage of your idealistic attitude.

For you, the world is love, and you want everyone to love *you* in particular. Your entire world revolves around being loved.

You perceive truth, and can sense when you are being deceived by others. But you are not above fooling yourself. You invite betrayal, at times, by an attitude so liberal that the reins are not only loosened, they are nonexistent.

Your desires are special in that you want to be special, young, and vigorous. It takes someone who makes you feel you are these things to claim your allegiance. And once that allegiance is won, you can be a pushover.

Listen, Sagittarius: there is no attempt here to belittle you. In truth, you deserve admiration. But your qualities of selection and discrimination leave more than a little to be desired. You choose, but not wisely. You can get what you want, but you don't always get what's good for you. You seek love, but you can get trouble instead.

The key, of course, is to see people in a true light. It is so necessary, in this area especially, for you to be alert, perceptive. You can be flattered, cajoled, made to believe you are the one-and-only—*even in the face of evidence to the contrary.*

This is not to say that you can't find the right person. It is to say that this seems more difficult for you than for the average person. There are triangles; there is deception. There are misunderstandings, and there can be significant age differences.

You are, as stated, idealistic and enthusiastic. You are not easy to comprehend, to analyze. You find it difficult to know yourself fully, especially in this area.

As a Sagittarian, man or woman, you are fiery, expressive and giving. Where love is concerned, you are generous. You hand your emotions over on a platter. You say, in effect, here I am, take me. You don't ask for much in return—except to be admired, appreciated, loved. You are curious about people—more so when you are emotionally involved with an individual. This, at first glance, is not unusual. But with you, there is an intensification of feeling. You are friendly and attractive, and members of the opposite sex confide in you. When someone strikes a responsive chord, it is you who may do the confiding. *And that is what you seek—a sharing; particularly a sharing of confidences.*

You are very long on giving advice. You want to be essential. Thus, you offer advice on health, emotions, money. Carried to extremes, this can be tiring. Realize that you are not loved for your advice. You are loved for your willingness to give, to be open, to be kind and generous and understanding. But not for advice; you are loved because of your ideals and your sense of adventure, for your spirit, for your aliveness, for your inspiration, but not for your advice.

Again and again, astrological experts say the worst partner for you is one with narrow, restricted views. You need someone who appreciates, accepts; someone who can be daring, and can share your zest for living.

You have so much you want to give that you attract some only too willing to accept. Like Leo, you enjoy being flattered. You believe, against your better judgment. Librans are especially adept at appealing to you in this manner, while Arians can cause you to throw logic out of the nearest window. Capricorns make you aware of money, but you could find these people too serious for your liking. You actually prefer someone who can learn from you, someone you can teach, persuade, influence and educate.

You are more affectionate than passionate, but you would not like this to be known. You are intense, but not necessarily sensuous. You are more intellectual than you are daring.

Love and sex, for you, mean an escape from routine, and a chance to soar emotionally. Because a meaningful relationship in this area represents freedom, you are unusual. Instead of feeling tied down, you feel released.

You find an outlet, you find light when you find someone to love. Frankly, love is your salvation. Without it travel, for instance, is no pleasure, it is a quest, a search—or a mere chore. With it, travel becomes a wondrous journey.

Listen: you are a romantic. This is why, at times, you give the impression of being flirtatious. You are basically gallant; you like compliments and you know how to give them. Sometimes, this results in a friendship or a relationship. You can get carried away, taken with the tide. You can be engulfed without having a chance to get your guard up: you believe that where love is concerned anything is possible.

You are dual in nature: on the negative side, you pretend. On the positive side, you are discreet. You don't care much about conventions, but you do care what people think. In a way, this is a dilemma: you want to fly high, above the trivial, above the mores of your time—but you also want to be a part of the world, leaving a good impression.

Obviously, you have a few problems, for the most part self-created; and especially where love and sex are involved. Your love nature can be domineering. You want to do the telling, the directing, the leading. You are martial in this area; you fight for what you want and you hurdle obstacles, including family and age. You can become involved with people who have serious problems, psychological and otherwise. This should be easy to understand. You attract those who need help. You draw to you people who need someone to lean on—and you don't object. In fact, you tend to revel in this kind of relationship. As long as you do remain in control of the situation, all is well. But when your partner veers from the course you have set, complications multiply.

Listen: you have no talent for making things easy for yourself. You have a knack for doing the opposite. You can be rash emotionally; you could give up much for speculation, for a hope, a dream. Those close to you can suffer because you reach out beyond what is immediately available.

You see beyond the immediate, but you are not always capable of being objective. You can "see" the way you want to, not the way your common sense dictates. Sometimes you simply throw aside your unique ability to get at the truth. You rationalize; you make excuses for people you love. You make excuses for your own actions. If you do this, you begin to be someone other than yourself. And that, Sagittarius, is where the trouble begins.

What is suggested from an astrological point of view? First, that you face the truth and carry on along realistic rather than imaginary lines. Second, that you hold on to what is good for you—and that you release what is destructive. Third, that you stop fooling yourself.

The Jupiter–Mars symbols, relating to love and sex for you, are exciting. The potential is tremendous—for good, or otherwise. These symbols indicate idealism, expansion, action and impulsiveness. How you want to give!

But, Sagittarius, in the *giving* you also are *taking*. The giving is not always the result of altruism. The giving is something you need. This is not contradictory.

The giving of advice, money and love is as essential to you as sleep, food and water. Instead of helping, you can cripple this way, making the object of your giving too dependent on you. When you perceive this course of events, pull up short. Analyze yourself. If you do this, you can prevent heartache and emotional chaos.

Like Cancer, you can be possessive. You want the person you love to move only in your sphere, at your direction. That's the effect of the Mars–Aries Fifth House. The Jupiter of Sagittarius is ultra-generous—but this becomes generosity to a fault in a very real sense when it leaps out of control.

If the lessons provided here are absorbed, Sagittarius, you will gain in stature and in actually achieving happiness in love. It isn't easy to advise someone to stop giving, to stop being generous. Actually, that is not the case. What you must stop is *giving for your own benefit.* If truly generous, you will give in a sensible manner—that is, sensible for yourself and for the individual in question. You will not give in order to create a dependent. You will, instead, give to create independence. Once independence is achieved, the relationship in question will become a truly meaningful one. This will be an open sesame to happiness.

You have a good sense of humor, which is perhaps one of the greatest assets anyone could seek. This enables you to laugh at your own foibles. And this quality is particularly attractive to the opposite sex. You can relieve tense situations through humor; and, if you temper humor with knowledge, you will never be in danger of becoming a bore.

It is fine to want to make a good impression. But, Sagittarius, you cannot be happy by taking actions in order merely to please others or to conform. Your sign symbolizes freedom, travel, education—and also love. There is no freedom without love in your sphere. There is no fulfillment without someone to share your triumphs—you simply are incomplete unless you care for someone special.

Your drives are definite. You'll have more than one opportunity for marriage. Love and marriage quite obviously represent serious business for you. You attract restless people. You attract people with psychological problems. Perhaps no more so than the average person, but those you attract confide and confess—to you.

You will find love. Perhaps you have already found it. But there are or will be complications. However, if that humor and sincere goodwill are permitted to shine through—the complications will never defeat you.

Avoid sarcasm; check yourself when you find that bickering is replacing conversation. Then this area of your life will glow. Your life will glow!

How You Relate to the Other Signs

Sagittarius is attracted to, and could marry, an Aries. You are harmonious in relation to Libra, Aquarius, Leo and Aries. Your sign is not well-aspected to Pisces,Virgo or Gemini and is considered neutral in relation to Scorpio, Capricorn, Taurus and Cancer.

Of course, this represents the briefest view of how you relate to other zodiacal signs. There are further details, nuances, and indications. Let's elaborate on some of the highlights.

Sagittarius with Aries

You are physically attracted to Aries; your creative abilities are stimulated by this relationship. The Mars of Aries and your Jupiter significator blend to enhance your mutual social activity and prospects for travel. The two signs—Aries and Sagittarius—are harmoniously aspected; the odds are great for a successful relationship.

You were born under a Fire sign; Aries belongs to the same element. A chord is struck, and a response is evinced. You *are* playing with fire when you're with an Aries. The association, for you, could mean children, love and marriage. There is no halfway here. This is far from a harmless flirtation.

You bring forth your creative resources with Aries. The Jupiter–Mars combination is excellent; it symbolizes a blend of direct action and long-range planning. A balance is struck and you can, with Aries, be contented on three levels: physical, mental and emotional.

No one is perfect, and there can be problems in this relationship. One is a tendency toward actions devoid of reason. Impulse tends to dominate. You tend, with Aries, to act first and think later. Complications, quite naturally, could arise. The physical attraction here could lead to a situation that creates embarrassment and pressure. Be sure you and Aries are free—legally and otherwise—to see each other, to maintain a relationship.

This is not something you can start and stop at Will. This game between Sagittarius and Aries is for high stakes. And once the chips are down, there may be no easy way out.

Sagittarius with Taurus

When you are with Taurus, there is emphasis on basic issues, health and work. Ideals are high and methods of serving the needs of others are stressed. With Taurus, you have a desire to produce beauty, to create an atmosphere that spells out harmony. Together, the signs are neutral, but there is a basic attraction. For the long haul, Taurus and Sagittarius make a good combination. You, Sagittarius, are fiery and idealistic; Taurus is earthy, practical and determined. This balances. The right amount of each could provide a winning mixture.

For you, Taurus could represent a stepping-stone, a pause, a breather. You may lean on Taurus; you may expect and demand the maximum degree of dependability from Taurus. You may, in fact, ask too much of Taurus.

Taurus performs services, helps make your life more comfortable. Taurus is a fixed sign and you are the opposite, being changeable and inconstant. Because of this, you could create a situation where you take Taurus for granted. Taurus will take only so much of this—and, finally, have enough.

With Taurus, you can create a product or service that has universal appeal. This is no small matter. It means the relationship can be valuable—in service to others and in profit to you.

To be with Taurus, you may have to burn the bridges of your past. This isn't always easy for you. In this case it may be worth it, however. Taurus will help you to take care of yourself. Taurus will aid in keeping you on an even keel.

Taurus will help you to make ideas work and will help you to utilize assets in a practical manner. It could be a rewarding relationship, especially over the long haul, in connection with future projects.

Sagittarius with Gemini

The accent in this association is on marriage, partnership, joint effort and public relations. With Gemini, you assume responsibility for your actions. You could get linked up with a Gemini in a permanent manner. The Mercury of Gemini combines with your Jupiter Solar significator to symbolize responsibility and reward. Gemini is quick, agile and versatile. Gemini can help you carry out your ideals.

You are attracted to Gemini, although the signs are in opposition. You are not opposite in nature. But Gemini has quick ideas, is a note-taker, while you philosophize and could be characterized as an essay-writer. There's a wide difference here, but the family is the same.

In a broad sense, there are many similarities between your sign and Gemini. In detail, however, there are vast differences. Gemini is restless and sees phases, perceives quick trends. You are willing to travel, but on longer journeys and at a more leisurely pace. You see long-range cycles, and Gemini could chide you for what appears to be procrastination.

Gemini is Air and you are Fire; getting together could either fan the flame, or extinguish it. Gemini makes you aware of public reactions. You get in the thick of things with Gemini. Your ideas become more direct, to the point. You have to move along to keep up with Gemini. You assume added responsibility, accept additional assignments and duties. But your income potential could rise as you receive greater recognition.

Marriage indications are strong here; the possibility of a union between Sagittarius and Gemini is a lively one. In a business alliance, Gemini and Sagittarius operate well and attract money. Together, these signs can produce commercial success.

That's the way it is with Sagittarius and Gemini: the accent is on partnership or marriage—either harmonious or the opposite.

Sagittarius with Cancer

Your Jupiter and the Cancer Moon significator combine to mean that you can make beautiful music with a Cancerian. It's a case of mutual attraction, although there are some problems, particularly in the financial area. Cancer affects that part of your Solar horoscope connected with legacies, the money of a mate or partner, the occult and hidden matters. Cancer is of the Water element and your sign belongs to the Fire Trinity. Fire and Water do not mix and, thus, you'll have to work hard to make this relationship click.

Cancer is concerned with money and security; your chief interests lie in travel, philosophy, writing and self-expression. There are bound to be obstacles, but if you are both mature, these can be overcome.

With Cancer, there is variety. There are changes, too. Your status is open to change. Cancer helps you make decisions. Cancer insists that you set a goal and that you pursue it. Cancer makes you aware of financial potential.

There is physical attraction here. Cancer relies on you for a cheering, optimistic note. You are drawn to Cancer in a mysterious manner. You are fascinated, and will attempt to fathom the depths of Cancer. You may never really know Cancer, but you could enjoy the attempt.

Together, Cancer and Sagittarius could come up with creative ideas. The key is to determine who is to direct operations. Cancer can be all business, and you can be wonderful at meeting and greeting the public. There tend to be financial disagreements. Cancer wants to conserve and you want to expend. The balance could be beneficial, but the key is to decide who sets policy.

With Cancer, you are entrusted with funds. Your capabilities are put on the line—and your investment acumen is tested.

Sagittarius with Leo

Leo affects that part of your Solar horoscope associated with journeys, including journeys of the mind; this means that Leo attracts and stimulates you. The Leo Sun and your Jupiter significator blend very favorably. The combination helps break down barriers or restrictions. These two Fire signs—Leo and Sagittarius—combine to mean that you two can set up guidelines, serve as inspirations to others. This is because, together, you two put idealism into action.

Leo aids you in transforming your noble notions to the drawing table, and, ultimately, to "the field."

Together, Jupiter and the Sun represent that which is, at one and the same time, inspiring and practical. You two can discover a way to hurdle objections and obstacles. Finances improve, and backing is obtained from sources that would be considered far removed from the immediate objective.

Obviously, Sagittarius and Leo are well-aspected, and the relationship has a great chance for success. The greatest obstacle to be faced here is impatience. There is intensity; there are high expectations. You may, Sagittarius, make the error of placing Leo on a pedestal. When Leo proves human, disillusion could set in. If mature, however, you will be prepared and understanding—and will take in stride various Leo imperfections.

There is physical attraction, but most of the stimulation here is apt to be on an intellectual level. Leo and Sagittarius form what might be termed a mutual admiration society. You share—and, when you feel a confidence has been violated, you retaliate. That might sound like the beginning of the end. Know this, Sagittarius, and realize that Leo is gregarious and possessive—Leo does not intend to take a back seat. Be sure, if you want this relationship to last, that Leo is the first to know things—and be lavish with your admiration and praise.

Sagittarius with Virgo

Virgo affects that part of your Solar horoscope associated with career, ambitions, prestige, and standing in the community. The Mercury of Virgo combines with your Jupiter to enable you to create money-making ideas. This is a good business relationship. The aspects overall, though, are less than favorable; there are conflicts, but Virgo does aid you in furthering your career or business ambitions.

You are more idealistic than is Virgo; natives of Virgo seem able to make you more practical in outlook. Virgo is basically earthy and is more concerned with results than with motives. This serves as a good balance with you; if you want to get a business off the ground, seek out a Virgo.

You tend to attract responsibility in association with Virgo; you also can achieve greater commercial success. Virgo stimulates your ambitions, but there is tension here. With Virgo, there are arguments. On a constructive level, these clear the air and bring you closer to your goals. On a negative level, the disagreements drain your energy.

You have lessons to learn from Virgo. You can have a fine relationship here. But it is tiring; it may be difficult to relax. There are pressures. For a time, you enjoy this; but after a while you may tire of the continual urging to "get ahead."

Virgo has ideas about health, general well-being and, with you, about how to succeed by really trying. Virgo may be too commercial for your taste.

Virgo is apt to be more physically attracted to you than the reverse. Generally, you gain where your career is concerned here. But emotionally there are obstacles; it's best to know this and be prepared.

Sagittarius with Libra

Libra is well-aspected to Sagittarius; the Venus of Libra combines with your Jupiter to bring about universal appeal in the two of you. Libra affects that part of your chart associated with friends, hopes, desires. There is definite attraction here, and there can also be material gain.

Beauty is highlighted: you need beautiful surroundings, motives, thoughts. There is also generosity, and this may be a pitfall.

With Libra, you tend to be extravagant. Your idealistic nature comes into focus: you give things away. In fact, you probably try to help those who are perfectly capable of aiding themselves.

Libra brings pleasure into your life. Libra is sensitive and this is a quality you deeply appreciate. Many of your hopes and wishes can be fulfilled with Libra. But you tend, also, to be impractical. You want to reach too far, too soon. You desire acclaim, and when it doesn't come rushing to your door, you are disillusioned.

Generally, there is pleasure here, fulfillment and a realization of many aspirations. With Libra, you attract people to you with their questions, problems. People confide in you. With the aid of Libra, you seem able to do something to help people, especially your friends.

For social activity, and for social work, Libra could be a perfect partner for you. For more practical or commercial enterprises, the relationship could fall short of the mark. Venus and Jupiter, to the eyes of an astrologer, represent a beautiful planetary setup. And there is an abundance of beauty, of light, of love, of good wishes and good intentions in this combination. But a solid base could be lacking.

With Libra, realize that one day the party will be over—practical issues will have to be faced. Be mature enough to know this, and you will enhance the odds for a successful relationship.

Sagittarius with Scorpio

Scorpio affects that part of your chart related to secrets, fears and confinement. The Pluto of Scorpio and your Jupiter form an unusual combination; there is great emphasis on secrecy and a need for discretion.

Clandestine meetings and activities appear to be associated with this relationship. Scorpio is a Water Sign and you belong to the Fire element; there are problems here, and a third person could be involved.

You are intrigued by the mystery, by the cloak-and-dagger aspects of this relationship. There is an element of deception, largely self-deception. With Scorpio, you could be seeing people and situations as you wish they would exist. For a time, you walk on clouds; then the reality of the situation comes to the fore and there is apt to be a reckoning.

You won't get something for nothing with Scorpio. The sooner you come to this realization, the better for all concerned. You deal with illusion here. There is usually a lack of solidity. If, early in the relationship, you see things in a realistic light, you'll have a better chance of success with intense Scorpio.

You are good for Scorpio where money is concerned. Scorpio lets you in on privileged information. You get behind the scenes with Scorpio. In the areas of motion pictures and television (and the theater), Scorpio is especially beneficial for you. Also, Scorpio is good for you in connection with fund-raising and charitable causes. You work well with Scorpio when the concern is for the welfare of others. But if your goal is to work toward personal gain, there could be difficulty.

Certainly, the combination of Sagittarius and Scorpio is intriguing. How long it lasts and how far it goes depend on the individuals involved.

Sagittarius with Sagittarius

With another Sagittarian, you have a desire for home and domesticity—but you also want a relationship free of flaws. You idealize and leave yourself open to disillusionment. There is basic understanding. You see many of your own traits, but usually the less desirable ones. This causes you to criticize because, perhaps subconsciously, you become aware of your own shortcomings. The relationship can be permanent, but not trouble-free. The success of it depends on the maturity of the Sagittarians involved. Your wandering days could be over with another Sagittarian; you could find a home.

The Sagittarius woman's decisions are swift. She is impulsive in affairs of the heart. What she admires most is a man of action. She needs a goal; it could be a trip, a book to read, or writing—whatever, the future is live and breathing for her, the future is a part of her because that's partly where she is.

She is exciting but can give the impression of being shy. She is a challenge that is difficult to resist. It's important to be basically honest with her. State your intentions; don't try to cover up with false promises. The more direct you are, the better it will be for you in this relationship. Once you win her confidence, once she feels loved, she can fulfill your fondest desires. She appreciates nature and likes men who like animals. She won't let you down if you confide in her; if you deceive her . . . look out!

The Sagittarius man would like you for his own, but wants greater freedom for himself. He isn't easy to understand completely, but is likely to be worth the effort. He is a natural actor and his life is apt to be one of travel, change, and excitement. He doesn't always take time to explain his actions. These are the times when he demands that you have faith in his judgment. He dislikes petty people. He wants you to learn, to grow, to gain as a result of your relationship with him. If you are honest, he can be won. If you are frank, he will respond in a sympathetic manner. You'll win him with color, charm, wit: you'll intrigue him by asking fantastic questions. He loses interest if you're conventional in your outlook, questions or ambitions. He wants the companionship of shared adventure. He wants to be independent—he is drawn to individuality and repelled by women who pretend to be something they are not.

Sagittarius with Capricorn

Capricorn affects that part of your Solar horoscope associated with money and personal possessions. The Saturn of Capricorn and your Jupiter help make you mutually intuitive where finances are concerned. You either get bogged down in this relationship, or you rise above petty details and obstacles. There seems to be little in between; you soar or sink.

Capricorn aids you in putting your talents on a business path; your product is made marketable through the aid of Capricorn. Saturn and Jupiter represent almost opposite ends of a pole: cheer and optimism (Jupiter) and restriction, discipline (Saturn). Together, this could add up to the kind of combination required for solid gain and profit.

Certainly, you are going to concentrate on financial gain with Capricorn. Natives of Capricorn are intrigued by you; your machinations are mysterious where Capricorn is concerned. If you and the Capricornian are mature, there is every reason to expect gain. Capricorn helps you in collecting data, in filling loopholes, in building that proverbial nest egg.

You object to many Capricorn characteristics; Capricorn tends to keep a part of himself secret and you are outgoing. You don't particularly enjoy being disciplined, and Capricorn can attempt to do this to you. But you can overlook a lot as you gain in a material sense.

You need some Capricorn in your life; everyone requires Saturn, like it or not. The relationship could grow and become meaningful. How long it lasts depends, of course, on the degree of mature understanding expressed by you and by Capricorn.

Sagittarius with Aquarius

Aquarius accents the part of your Solar horoscope that is connected with ideas, relatives, short journeys, quick decisions and intellectual curiosity. The Uranus of Aquarius and your Jupiter significator combine in a manner favorable for excitement, adventure, sudden change and travel. There is attraction here, and the signs are favorably aspected.

Your love of change and travel is fulfilled to a great degree with Aquarius. These people are exciting, different, concerned with subjects considered radical or unorthodox. This intrigues, fascinates you.

A drawback here is a tendency to scatter forces, to try being in too many places at once. With no discipline, confusion is apt to run rampant. The key is concentration on the basic issues. Otherwise, the pace is dizzying and the experience is like a merry-go-round. If you don't want to go in circles, decide at the outset where you are headed and why.

Aquarius helps you investigate; encourages you to write. Aquarius stimulates you mentally and helps you make meaningful decisions. If you are seeking a humdrum existence, Aquarius is not your cup of tea. If you seek excitement and change, then you have probably found the right individual in Aquarius.

In the problem department, there are relatives who might object to the relationship—on one or both sides. There is a strong magnetism that draws Sagittarius and Aquarius together. But the relationship is tiring, the pace is fast, the objectives can be blurred.

You can succeed with Aquarius if you are not afraid to change some basic concepts. It is necessary to be daringly flexible. You must also be versatile. Life takes on a bright hue with Aquarius. You can be happy—if you don't burn the candle at both ends.

Sagittarius with Pisces

You may get a new outlook as a result of your relationship with a Pisces. Pisces affects that part of your Solar horoscope connected with home, long-range projects and basic security. The Neptune of Pisces blends with your Jupiter significator to open new horizons. You review your past and accept new views through Pisces. The two signs are not favorably aspected. This is a case of Fire (Sagittarius) and Water (Pisces). There are, naturally, problems in getting the elements to mix. But there is interest and it is a good combination where home, property, real estate and long-range security enter the picture.

Like Scorpio, Pisces has an aura of mystery that you find attractive. You want to get to the bottom of mysteries, to solve puzzles, to add to your holdings. Pisces, in turn, regards you as an asset toward the fulfillment of ambitions.

Both you and Pisces seem to have individual motives or goals in this aspect of the relationship. It is not a selfless one. There are reasons for actions on both your parts, and if you are mature enough to know this, then there is more of a chance for ultimate success. There could be conflict as to who is running the show. With a Pisces, you tend to be independent, slightly selfish.

When you are ready to settle down, to change or take a new view, then Pisces may be right for you. Otherwise, you could feel tied down, restricted, and even abused. On the brighter side, Pisces could make you a good home and could help you make investments that enhance your long-range security. Neptune and Jupiter could spell romance, but there is also a puzzling aspect. You might, with Pisces, be constantly wondering just where you stand and where you are going next.

Capricorn

December 22 - January 19

The Fifth Sector of a chart is related, among other things, to sex. Your Fifth Solar House is Taurus, which gives us some indications about sex and love in relation to you.

With Taurus on the cusp of your Fifth House, your needs are basic as well as complex. You are possessive in the sense that Cancer is, jealous in the way that Leo can be. Taurus is associated with Venus, the Venus ruler of your Fifth House. Combined with your Saturn significator, it reveals that your emotions often are an open book. And, even more often, a closed one. In the sex and love area, you are vulnerable. You do communicate your feelings. Love is life for you.

You obviously are somewhat of a puzzle. You are ambitious, but patient. You feel, deep within yourself, that you have a link with destiny. You are convinced that time is on your side. Because of this, you are determined and persistent. You are able to get up, when set back, and continue the battle. You are not ready to give up your principles, but you are willing to retreat. You are willing to lose battles in order to win major objectives. In matters of sex, you are deadly serious; you require love as some people require money or food or water. Without love, life is a diminished force for you. Sex is a basic for you and you are confused by those who assign it a secondary role.

Being of the Tenth Sign, at the top of the zodiac, you constantly have a goal—something to strive for, to attain. This doesn't make you the easiest person to understand. You often have a faraway look. You seek. You want to capture wisdom when, in truth, trying to cram or force knowledge often has the opposite effect. You can chase it instead of capturing it.

The combination of Saturn (Capricorn) and Venus (your Fifth House indicator) provides planetary symbols which, in turn, cast greater light on your sexual attitudes. Venus represents love; Saturn, discipline. Saturn stands for patience and Venus for luxury. Capricorn is a sparse sign and Taurus (your Fifth House sign) is a full one, meaning that someone influenced by it may be inclined to excess. This tells us that you are an unusual, often contradictory combination. You can discipline yourself but will not tolerate others trying to do it for you. You want to call the shots, outline the programs, decide when to stop and go. When someone you love attempts to impose a program, you rebel. You are, as a matter of fact, a natural rebel; not only in matters of sex, but in various areas of society.

You attract many affairs of the heart—you constantly become involved. You experiment, you deprive yourself to the point where you are hungry enough to devour anyone. You consume yourself in the sense that you are never *completely* satisfied. This is a matter of your own doing. You can never achieve happiness until you realize that you are hurting yourself; it is you who does the flogging, the denying. It is your Saturn side disciplining your Venus one.

When this gets out of balance, out of sync, there are emotional reverberations. You drive—you find paradise, and then you become restless, you retreat. *You find love and you find fault.* You give much to people who are only superficially interested. You *take* from those who are only too willing to sacrifice on your behalf. It is all, very obviously, turned around then and mixed up, confused. It should be that you give to the worthy and take from those who are only playing games.

Your Seventh or marriage House is Cancer, associated with the Moon. The Moon, Saturn (your significator) and Venus (Fifth House ruler) paint a picture of a need for warmth, a tendency to squander affections and a tremendous feeling of *insecurity.* You constantly reach out for love. You feel you want permanency, but you do almost everything to provide roadblocks to permanent relationships.

Once you recognize these contradictions for what they are, the better for all concerned. What, then, are they these roadblocks to fulfillment in the area of love and sex? We go back to the word "insecure." They are an attempt—these roadblocks—to protect yourself from reality. You want to be permanent, but fear being tied down.

Why? Again quite a question. And the answer is contained in your inner conviction of your own worth. This means, Capricorn, that your goals are sky-high; the *permanency* you desire is *recognition.* But when you receive that recognition (love) from one individual, you set your sights higher. You are not satisfied with the status quo. Then, there are times when you feel that you have arrived, but in this arrival you have frightened the very person who gives you that secure feeling. The positions are reversed. The search begins anew. It is a circle—but you can ride it with pleasure instead of pain once you understand its workings.

Capricorn women seek protection. Women under this sign often substitute tears for fulfillment. But until they become mature, they seek relationships which they should know will result in emotional bruises. Capricorn men possess a strong protective instinct—later in life they fulfill their ambitions and attract women who seek material security. Capricorn men and women possess high ideals, but they tend to wander in all directions at once. This leaves their partners with a feeling of being lost.

Capricorn, in this area, is cautious about revealing true feelings. But when the armor is removed, it is all the way. Capricorn does not make small mistakes. When Capricorn gives, it is all or nothing. When it is to the wrong person, then the loss or mistake is a great one.

Put succinctly, Capricorn is passionate. That's why natives of this sign are cautious. They know they cannot give halfway. They inwardly realize that, once committed, they will go all the way. Young Capricorns are particularly aware of this fact. That's why they give the appearance of being aloof. But once the guard is down, once the emotions are exposed—Capricorn is warm, giving, at times violent with expression. This being the case, we can realize why Capricorn seems cautious, selective, afraid to let go.

Yet, until you—born under this sign—can learn to let go, there is no real fulfillment. What you must do is to decide well, and then give. You should be selective, but once the decision is made, give. What you must also do is to realize that *giving* means receiving and understanding, too.

Realize that perfection is an ideal rarely—if ever—achieved. What I ask you to do is not to feel the world is coming to an end when you do make a mistake. Relax! Then the sex and love area of your life is given a chance to glow with the satisfaction you so earnestly seek.

Listen: you are sensuous, no matter what some of the textbooks state. You are sometimes "cold with desire," as I have written. And you can be more than a match for anyone in the love and sex area.

Some say you are more dutiful than loving. But, in actuality, you become dutiful when your affection is misplaced. That is, when your love is wasted, given to someone who doesn't appreciate it—that is when love, for you, is transformed into duty. You become the dutiful mate rather than the loving one. But, if you heed the advice about being selective, there will be no need for this painful transition.

Without love, all of life becomes a routine, a duty; with love, where you are concerned, there is life and it is worth living.

You are very good at managing the affairs of others, but could fall down on the job where your own are concerned. This means that you are farsighted enough to sense potential and to advise others to do something about it. With yourself, there is a tendency to delay, to put off, to permit opportunity to fly away. Correct this and your entire life will change—love will become a reality rather than a dream.

You can be the power behind the throne. And you do have a taste for power. Perhaps achievement would be a better word; you want to achieve, and when you love someone you want that individual up there, on top—you make room at the top.

Your disposition is not even; it is subject to ups and downs, featuring laughter and tears. You are possessive. You love the idea of being in love; you cherish being in love. The key is not to confuse being in love with love with being in love with an individual. If this confusion is not avoided, you could be a victim of Saturn rather than the recipient of what joyous Venus offers.

You are lusty in this area; that cold exterior becomes flaming warm. You will sacrifice anything for love. You win fight for love—and you will gain your objective, usually, no matter how long it takes for this to occur.

Being born under the natural tenth zodiacal sign, with Saturn as your significator, you enjoy playing the role of manager. In the love area, you could also tend to dominate intimate moments. That is, you seem to want to control when and where intimate, tender moments are to occur. Perhaps a plainer way of stating this is to say you manage rather than respond. You should, quite obviously, give yourself over to spontaneity. When you manage and plan and calculate—no matter how lofty your motives—you defeat much of your pleasure.

You think too much! Your conscious mind battles the subconscious; you are so busy thinking, asking, probing, wondering why, that what should be happening naturally often does not occur at all. If you are a classic Capricorn, the import of these words should be clear, direct and obvious.

You are always willing to assume responsibility for your acts. You don't attempt to shirk it by claiming that emotions took over, or that you were not thinking clearly. What you do—for whatever reasons—you do. That is your attitude—that it is done, I did it, and it is my music to face. This is admirable, Capricorn, except when others—sensing this—try to shove more than your share of any burden on your shoulders. That is another reason why you must be selective. You tend to draw to you people who lean and deprive and sap your psychological energy.

Marriage, for you, represents security and unity. You feel that marriage should be the uniting of two people into one—and you are selfish about that concept. You don't want to modify it. Because you are stern about this concept—that marriage is literally the welding together of two people—marriage can be delayed for you. You are apt to be accused of having a one-track mind in this area, but your motives and ideals are constructive. As a woman, you can help your man achieve his potential. As a man, you can elevate the standing in the community of the person you love.

Marriage, for you, represents a kind of warm security; it represents a chance to build, to create, to begin anew. For you, marriage is the excitement of self-recognition; you come alive with marriage, although you could marry more than once, and later in life.

How wrong those people are who consider you cold-blooded! You are inwardly warm, hopeful *and näive.* Your ideals propel you to great heights. Often reality acts like an anchor, dragging you down to the depths. That's why you can be happy and sad, almost at the same time. Almost simultaneously, you can be elated, then disappointed; a kind of ambivalent mood is sometimes associated with sex and love for you.

Your love nature is intense; you become totally committed to the object of your affections. You give; you are made vulnerable because you wear your heart on your sleeve for that special individual. You can, in this area, do plenty to punish yourself. You can become involved with people who take rather than give, use you, lean on you, confide problems but are reluctant to share joys.

Your memory is long: if someone you adore cheats, you are not likely to forgive that person, even if it appears that you are doing so on the surface. You expect others to live up to your ideals. The fact that they do not always do so explains some of the disappointments which dot your life in this area.

For you, anything is possible. Your sign—Capricorn—is the top one, the natural Tenth House, representing power, time and achievement. Your Fifth House (sex and love) is associated with Venus, the planet of love. Saturn and Venus make a formidable combination. It is a matter of hard reality against dreams, of restriction contrasted with limitless opportunity for pleasure. If proper balance is achieved, your potential for happiness is tremendous.

You can be vindictive. You don't easily forgive someone who takes advantage of circumstances in this area. That long, timeless memory comes into play; you bide your time. Love can turn into hate. What was an object of affection can become one of scorn. You are not really one to play games with in the emotional area.

When you love—if your trust is not abused—you love long and well. When you love, your life is vibrant: there is an air of expectation, of discovery; joy replaces an apparent moroseness which often characterizes you.

Sex and love—for you these represent responsibility, the giving of life. They represent your creative being. Without them, you are less than half alive.

How You Relate to the Other Signs

Capricorn is harmonious in relation to Scorpio, Pisces, Taurus and Virgo. You are physically attracted to Taurus and delighted by Scorpio; you could marry Cancer and you laugh a lot with Pisces. Your aspirations are often tied up with Virgo. Aries and Libra could represent problems, while Aquarius could cost you money. Capricorn is considered neutral in relation to Sagittarius, Aquarius, Gemini and Leo. Sagittarius, though, represents the possibility that you could be involved in a clandestine affair.

Of course, this represents the briefest view of how you relate to other zodiacal signs. There are further details, nuances, indications: let's elaborate on some of the highlights.

Capricorn with Aries

With Aries, you deal in practical, concrete matters. Aries is a great teammate when combined with you in real estate and property matters. Aries touches the part of your Solar horoscope that is connected with your home and with projects which affect your future security. Aries opens up to you . . . talks to you . . . but you can count on Aries in the future rather than immediately. That is, if you are seeking long-range results, Aries is your person. But not so if you are seeking the immediate, if you are looking for quick or flash results.

Aries with you indicates the future—and, for you, the relationship is serious. Listen, Capricorn: don't think you can dabble or experiment with Aries. The relation is apt to prove lasting, for real—solid and not tinsel, responsible and not superficial. You can make money with Aries. You can successfully invest with Aries. You could marry Aries because Aries awakens in you a desire for home, family, property, land, something solid on which to rest. That's how Aries affects Capricorn.

Listen—it is an interesting combination, your Saturn and the Mars of Aries—Fire and Earth, action and depth. You inspire Aries to great heights. You awaken ambition in Aries. For you, Aries is an anchor in the best sense; something to look forward to: the future seen as warm instead of terrifying.

There is attraction here—and there are problems. Both of you learn as a result of the relationship. The signs—Capricorn and Aries—are not well-aspected. But each builds the character of the other. You can expect discipline and responsibility as a result of your relationship with Aries. But there is mutual attraction and there could be financial reward. And this could aid in alleviating some of the problems between Aries and Capricorn.

Capricorn with Taurus

With you and a Taurus, there are creative forces that are activated. There is change, travel, variety, the spark of physical attraction. The two signs are harmonious and the relationship could be very beneficial.

Listen, Capricorn: with Taurus you are aware of romance, of popularity, of personal magnetism, of creative resources. You come to life with Taurus. You want to communicate and Taurus helps you break the ground, cut through red tape, and helps you shake off lethargy.

Taurus affects that part of your Solar horoscope associated with love, romance, children and creative endeavors, too. Taurus encourages you, gives you a new lease on life. The combination of Taurus and Capricorn is favorable. You are attracted to Taurus, but Taurus coincides with restlessness, and creates unhappiness if you insist on maintaining the status quo. Taurus, where you are concerned, involves variety. Taurus represents self-evaluation. Taurus, for you, symbolizes your potential, your creative urge.

The Venus of Taurus combines with your Saturn to produce a blend of beauty and discipline. There is little question that, with Taurus, your experience is utilized in a manner that brings beauty and emotional reward. Also, with Taurus, there is activity connected with children. In general, the relationship is rewarding and, with a fair amount of effort on your part, and on the part of Taurus, the end result is happiness.

I would say to you, Capricorn, that a little Taurus the Bull in your life would be a favorable thing. The rest is up to you!

Capricorn with Gemini

Gemini affects that part of your Solar horoscope associated with work, health and special services. The Mercury of Gemini and your Saturn combine to produce discipline, determination and an awareness of details which brings basic goals closer to reality.

That is a key in your association with Gemini—reality. This is rather odd because Gemini can be flighty and almost the opposite of realistic. Nevertheless, combined with Capricorn, the native of Gemini is apt to turn over a new leaf.

That is not always exactly the case. But what does happen with you and Gemini is that the Gemini wit, skill and versatility is aimed at a specific goal, is disciplined: the energy is channeled toward accomplishment. Thus, with Gemini, you have one who can serve basic needs and who can help you with your job and with essential chores.

For Gemini, you represent responsibility and the promise of reward. Capricorn and Gemini are very different; it is this difference that each could find attractive.

Saturn (Capricorn) and Mercury (Gemini) make an intriguing combination.

Mercury is quick, flitting and flirting. Saturn stands for discipline, time, testing, restriction. When natives of these signs get together, Saturn tends to dominate, which means that Gemini bends, becomes more practical.

For you, Capricorn, a relationship with Gemini leads to renewed interest in health, work and recreation. Gemini helps you gain a new foothold in that you become interested in everyday affairs, current events and in what you are doing in the way of basic tasks. Gemini is apt to be attracted to you in a more emotional manner than you are to him or her. Gemini serves your needs, helps build your strength and has a genuine concern for your physical welfare.

Capricorn with Cancer

In connection with Cancer, the emphasis for you is on marriage, public relations, partnerships and legal affairs. You are attracted to Cancer, but, again, much in the manner that opposites attract opposites. Listen, Capricorn where people born under Cancer are concerned, you are encouraged to enter new areas. You express greater independence. You bring forth original and creative methods. Your Saturn and the Cancer Moon spell out intensity of purpose. You are apt to kick over the traces, to begin anew. Cancer touches that part of your Solar horoscope which makes you aware of the public, of public reactions.

Cancer brings publicity, recognition for your efforts. Cancer, as we say, also affects that section of your chart related to marriage. You could be permanently tied, enduringly connected to Cancer. There is a part of you reflected in Cancer, just as a part of Cancer is reflected in your sign, Capricorn.

Cancer and Capricorn are signs in opposition to each other. But, along with the opposition, there is definite attraction. If you want to come out of your shell, if you want to advertise and publicize . . . then you've found the right person in Cancer.

For you, Cancer represents a chance for added independence of thought, action. For new starts, Cancer is your perfect partner. Cancer encourages you to pioneer, to utilize your experience in a daring manner. Both Cancer and Capricorn are aware of security—together they can make significant financial gains. There is much in the Cancer native that appeals to you. You have a great deal in common. Habit patterns could develop which can make this relationship a most significant one.

Capricorn with Leo

Leo touches that part of your chart related to the money of other people. Leo creates interest for you in the occult, the hidden, in tarot cards and palmistry and extrasensory perception. Leo amazes and intrigues you: Leo can become a part of you almost before you know it.

The Leo Sun and your Saturn spell out universal appeal. Plans are big and many are attracted. In a business involving financial advising, Leo would make a perfect partner for you. With Leo, you inspire confidence. Others are drawn to you with problems, questions, plans and campaigns.

You are attracted to Leo because, in contrast to your reserved makeup, Leo is outgoing, flamboyant, a natural showman. Leo also introduces you to areas which are hidden, covered, mysterious. The relationship is not free of misunderstandings, separations, obstacles. But it could be a lasting one.

With you and Leo, there is interest and concern over legacies, the property of deceased people. You make future plans with Leo. There is apt to be more fun in anticipating than there is joy in the current, the "now" of the relationship. The two signs have so much *not* held in common that there are bound to be disputes.

The people you attract are not likely to be especially appreciated by Leo. However, Leo brightens the bleakness of Saturn; Leo could provide incentive for you to engage in creative endeavors. For a time, there is physical attraction. How long this lasts depends, of course, on you and the individual Leo.

This is not an ideal relationship. But it could be a meaningful one and it could change your outlook, to say nothing of your life pattern. Generally, Leo represents a key to unique experiences for you—some happy, others the opposite.

If it's challenge you seek—laughter mingled with tears—then Leo is for you.

Capricorn with Virgo

Virgo affects the part of your Solar horoscope related to long journeys, publishing, communications, and education. The Mercury of Virgo and your Saturn combine to indicate concerted effort toward long-range goals. The signs are harmonious; both belong to Earth. Virgo can get you moving, encourage you to improve techniques and to enlarge your personal and professional horizons.

You could, with Virgo, feel a pinch of restriction. You respond by trying to break from routine, from established patterns. This can be constructive if you know what you're doing. Otherwise, you merely rock the boat of your security.

For any publishing venture, Virgo is beneficial. For travel plans and actual journeys, Virgo is a wonderful partner. For higher education and self-improvement, Virgo is a definite asset. What you must do, in conjunction with Virgo, is to prepare a solid base. Otherwise, you go off on wild-goose chases; you move aimlessly in a circle of confusion. With proper preparation, there can be real accomplishment. But this requires patience and discipline. Know this and plan; go over details, be observant, check the fine print and read between the lines.

Virgo can help you attain, can make your aspirations practical and encourage you to express your views. Virgo is especially beneficial for you in any political or popularity poll. Virgo helps you articulate your needs, ideas, goals. Most important, Virgo aids you in preparing, outlining, and planning.

With Virgo, you can go far—you can break through to progress. Most certainly, this relationship deserves your very best efforts.

Capricorn with Libra

Libra affects that part of your chart related to career, ambitions, prestige. The Venus of Libra and your Saturn combine to promote change, creativity, travel, physical attraction. Libra awakens your ambitions and your sense of power, authority. You want to impress Libra, and this desire can be transformed into ambition.

Your standing in the community is elevated with Libra. You appreciate Libra's love of the arts, of the finer things in life. Libra looks to you as an example of solidity and as a potential good provider.

Libra can help you make important career contacts. Libra helps offset your reserved nature. A Libran helps others to know your special capabilities. With Libra, you can advance. You can gain promotions and you can run your own business.

The two signs are not favorably aspected; a challenge is there, and so is pressure. All is not easy; Libra pushes you, chides you, makes you bring out the best in yourself in professional matters. For gaining prestige, Libra is excellent for you; for special community projects and for initiating a business deal, Libra is also beneficial. Venus helps tone down your Saturn, making it more palatable to others. Thus, despite the unfavorable aspect between the signs, Libra can be of value where you are concerned.

There are problems here. But there also are obvious benefits. Libra is just; Libra will trumpet your talents, abilities. But, it appears, Libra is apt to be better for you in professional activities than when it comes to a strictly personal relationship.

Capricorn with Scorpio

Scorpio affects that part of your Solar horoscope that is related to desires and friends. You harmonize with Scorpio, and you can fulfill many of your wishes in conjunction with a native of this sign. The Pluto significator of Scorpio combines with your Saturn to break restrictions, to permit greater freedom of thought and action.

Both signs—Capricorn and Scorpio—are intense and ambitious. There are problems, but harmony could prevail. This depends on an agreement concerning basic goals. A Scorpio can enhance your versatility, get you going and help correct a tendency for you to be morose. You travel with Scorpio; you express your views, write and make numerous and exciting social contacts.

Physical attraction exists—you are drawn to Scorpio. There is much activity and there are numerous occasions for laughter. This strikes many of your friends as odd, since neither you nor Scorpio are particularly noted for a light attitude. With Scorpio, however, there is opportunity for you to come out of yourself. With a Scorpio, you shake off lethargy. You emerge and begin to let others know of your abilities, hopes, and aspirations.

You often confuse Scorpio, but this works as an exciting challenge. Scorpio helps you attain many things, but most of all, Scorpio aids you in self-discovery. You'll learn here what it is you seek—and how to get it.

The Pluto-Saturn combination is powerful; these natives together respect the past but insist on building their own traditions. Thus, with Scorpio, you will gain renewed confidence. There could be some violent arguments; but the "making up" should compensate amply for the quarreling.

The potential for this relationship is great. You should give it a try.

Capricorn with Sagittarius

Sagittarius affects that part of your Solar horoscope associated with secrets, restrictions, fears, doubts, clubs, organizations and clandestine or behind-the-scenes affairs. The Jupiter of Sagittarius combines with your Saturn to produce a combination that is favorable for teaching, for the bringing to the fore of radical ideas, unusual methods, occult principles and far-out subjects.

Sagittarius and Capricorn are regarded as neutral, but generally the natives of this Jupiter-ruled sign must be considered as favorable to you. There are secrets, and there are maneuvers designed to evade detection, but there are also benefits as a result of your both being able to skip over red tape and to gain major points without recourse to middlemen.

Jupiter is a wonderful antidote to Saturn; the combination represents cheer as opposed to discipline, expansion in contrast to restriction. Thus, there is balance—and there is also romance. Perhaps it would be more accurate to say that your relationship with Sagittarius produces *intrigue.* You might never know quite where you stand. In a sense, this is a challenge. In another sense, it can cause frustration.

Challenge, frustration and romance are featured when Capricorn and Sagittarius get together. If you are engaging in a motion picture or television project, a Sagittarius is especially good for you. If you are raising funds for charitable organizations, Sagittarius is beneficial. But if you want everything out in the open, Sagittarius may not be the right person for you. With Sagittarius, there are secrets and you may find yourself telling lies as a result of the relationship.

Sagittarius will take you behind the scenes, on the inside. You might find the association worth all of the disadvantages it could present.

Capricorn with Capricorn

With another Capricorn, you tend to make wonderful plans, but they could lack solidity. The relationship leaves much to be desired, though it could succeed if each Capricornian is determined to carry through on his or her promises. In actuality, it may be a case of too many chiefs and not enough Indians. Obviously, this means both want to lead, direct and dominate. A decision must be made as to which one is boss. Once this is done, the relationship could flourish.

Capricorn with Aquarius

Aquarius affects that part of your chart related to income potential and possessions. The Uranus of Aquarius blends with your Saturn significator to promote new ideas, pioneering efforts, and added independence of thought and action.

With Aquarius, you are more aware of money and how to obtain it. The Saturn-Uranus blend is one that topples the past and builds for the future. You appreciate the suddenness, the drama of Aquarius; it helps offset your tendency to be ultra-serious. With Aquarius, you become concerned with the future rather than brooding over what might have been. The combination here is not perfect; but very few things are without flaws. There can be breaks, interruptions in the relationship. But there is every chance for your reuniting after a separation.

There is conflict over who is to call the signals, you or Aquarius. This should be settled, not in an arbitrary manner, but through trial and error. Obviously, a great deal of mature understanding is required if this relationship is to flower and grow.

Aquarius, although often in conflict with you, finds you fascinating. Live up to the image. Don't tell all you know; maintain an air of mystery. For you, Aquarius represents a chance to add to your security, financial and otherwise. Aquarius helps set the tone, provides a sense of direction. Aquarius and Capricorn make a fine team for new pioneering projects. The original is accented; new twists are featured; profit is obtained through the providing of unique products.

The big question is who will be boss; it is an issue that, ultimately, must be settled. If it is, in a satisfactory manner, the least result of this combination will be more money in the bank for you, Capricorn.

Capricorn with Pisces

Pisces affects that part of your chart related to short journeys, ideas as opposed to long-range philosophy, relatives, and your ability to adjust to changing situations. The Neptune of Pisces and your Saturn significator combine to promote domestic stability, a keen desire for a home and family. The signs—Pisces and Capricorn—are favorably aspected and the odds are great for a constructive relationship.

In your association with a Pisces, there appear to be numerous trips of the short variety in the offing. There are ideas, there is experimentation—and there is, very likely, a scattering of forces. Pisces can make you laugh. Pisces can charm you. Pisces, when combined with Capricorn, could add up to marriage, home, domesticity. There are close dealings with members of your families involved in this relationship. Pisces regards you as a friend and admires your realistic attitude. You are intrigued by the Piscean intuitive intellect. You never quite fathom the whole Pisces, but the challenge keeps you interested.

Neptune and Saturn make a good blend; one is imaginative, and the other is practical. With mature effort, a fine balance can be achieved. The relationship here is good. Much, of course, depends on the complete horoscope. But, basically, the aspect between Capricorn and Pisces is a sextile; under this aspect people tend to stay married to each other. In buying a home, you do well with the aid of Pisces. In building a project for the future, on a solid base, you do very well with Pisces. Natives of this sign could tire you, keep you on the go—but it is unlikely that you would object. There are too many laughs—and, although there could be some tears, your mutual humor prevails.

This is an excellent relationship to pursue.

Aquarius

January 20 - February 18

The Fifth Sector of a chart is related, among other things, to sex. Your Fifth Solar House is Gemini, which gives us some indications about sex and love in relation to you. Gemini is associated with the planet Mercury. The planets Uranus (your Solar significator) and Mercury combine to give us a symbolic picture of some of your attitudes toward sex and love.

Listen: Uranus is progressive, while Mercury is the planet of communications. You are very much aware of touch, feeling, tenderness. You cannot obtain real gratification, fulfillment, without *mind-to-mind* contact. No part of the horoscope stands alone; there are twelve sections, covering every area of life. There is a blend. The Fifth House is sex, but how it "operates" is dependent on the other eleven sectors, the complete personality, the horoscope. Thus, being born under Aquarius, know that you are not going to respond on a purely physical level. Mind-to-mind contact, in your case, is as important as actual physical contact. Yet, touch—in the literal physical sense—is important, but to evoke response it must be combined with *tenderness.*

Obviously, you are sensitive; you need to be regarded as an individual, not as a sexual object. One of your greatest mistakes, Aquarius, is a tendency to compromise in this area—to comply, please or apparently satisfy your partner.

This is a mistake because, when you permit the bar of your own principles to come down, you forego your *natural* role. What is that role? It is that of *teacher.* You are the instructor in the sense that you set an example; an example of high standards. If you compromise, you lose pleasure and, ultimately, your partner does, too, through lack of respect. To give and receive joy in the area of sex and love, you must adhere to your own standards. To compromise is to water down opportunities for happiness. Realize this and respond accordingly.

Aquarius, you do exhibit a tendency to lower your own standards here. This invites unpleasant situations. You attract people to you only too willing to use or take advantage of your basically altruistic nature. Many times, you are encouraged *for a purpose.* You are susceptible to flattery (as is your opposite sign, Leo). You make excuses for people you love, you deny yourself in order to provide greater satisfaction for others. In any other area or department of life, this could be regarded as idealism. But in sexual relations this could lead to problems, possibly emotional trouble. As Evangeline Adams, the great astrologer, once stated, you should never take the advice of others against your own intuition or judgment. And I have found it a fact, Aquarius, that some of your greatest difficulties come through being misguided because of a desire to serve . . . and, in this area in particular, because of a desire to please at the cost of denying your own pleasure principles.

Your sign is one of special qualities. You are an individual in such a real sense that to be anything but yourself is a grievous error. Being an individual does create problems. Your special problem, in the area of sex, is one of restlessness, a feeling that you need to understand and be understood to a greater degree. You tend to be pleased on the outside, but seldom are you completely happy on the inside.

The Uranus–Mercury symbolism is one of reaching, trying to envelope the world. You desire excitement, travel. You are creative, but often your efforts are superficial. Because of this, you attract people who, in their turn, scatter their forces, who are not constant. Your own actions, in other words, can bring people to you who create unhappy situations.

Through the use of astrological technique, we are able to provide these insights. But the purpose is self-improvement and ultimate happiness. Plainly, the insights are just a start. What you do about them, how you *respond,* is really of major importance. It does no good to know the traffic light is red if you are going to cross the street anyway.

It is to your advantage to have these revelations only if you do something about them—or at least make an effort to do something. Being an Aquarian, you are apt to be more responsive to astrology than is the average individual. Because of this, you are more likely to be aided.

You can help yourself, through sound astrology, by a fairly simple process. First, self-examination is required. Are the statements made here correct? If so, even if to a degree of, let us say seventy percent, then do something about it.

Take one step at a time. Apply yourself. Be thorough as opposed to flashy. Climb from the bottom to the top instead of trying to leap to the top in one gigantic stride. This will give you a stronger, broader base and result in greater self-confidence. In turn, this earns you respect and brings to you partners who possess the sincerity you so sorely require.

This may sound odd, Aquarius, but (at times) you seem intent on hurting yourself, on hurting people you love. That's your negative side. On the positive side, you are willing to try new techniques, to experiment, to provide partners with the spice of life.

You are, as has been stated, intellectual but stubborn. You are all for progress, but in your own time and way. You want to please, but expect so much that you often "frighten" your partner. I mean, Aquarius, that you expect so much in the way of *response* that others find themselves concentrating on this aspect rather than enjoying themselves to the degree necessary to make that response genuine and spontaneous. Do you recognize yourself?

The sign on the cusp of your Seventh or marriage sector is Leo, associated with the Sun. The sign on the cusp of your Fifth or sexual sector is Gemini, associated with Mercury. Your own planetary significator is Uranus. Now we have three symbols to work with: Uranus, Mercury and the Sun. This trinity, properly understood, provides lessons that can make your life a happier, more complete one.

Let's face one basic fact: you need bright, responsive, alert, *feeling* partners. If you do not have one, start finding the reason why the lack exists. In your sexual attitudes, give of yourself in a natural manner. Get rid of emotional armor. Don't make excuses for others; don't talk down, or act down, to others—above all, do not lower your own standards.

Don't be patronizing. Realize others *want to learn from you,* and your self-respect quotient will rise—and so will the heights of your own pleasure.

Be demanding, but not only of friends: also of one with whom you are *emotionally* involved. But be demanding in the sense that a creative teacher is demanding. Then and only then will you be fulfilling your role to the greatest extent—the extent that leads to physical pleasure and emotional satisfaction.

You are the kind of individual who needs lessons and statements driven home, emphasized. That's why, at times in this analysis, I have deliberately attempted to sound a sort of "Johnny-One-Note." That note could bring harmony to your life.

It is a note which sounds out and rings for you to be the master of your own fate, especially in this area. The master of your own fate: that fate could take you to the highest rung of the ladder. But, without a fulfilled emotional life, you'll find it a difficult climb.

The way toward fulfillment lies in adhering to the highest principles, and standards. The way lies in finding a partner who responds, who is anxious to learn and please and experiment. The way to fulfillment does *not* lie in attracting frightened people who know only that they have a duty to perform.

Your concepts must be grand ones; the person you attract can live up to your expectations if you are discriminating, perceptive. You not only deserve the best, you *need* quality. You need the best if you are to be happy.

Sex and love—for Aquarius these often become intellectualized. But the need (as for Capricorn) is for actual participation. You get nowhere in this area if you analyze it to death. You can deceive yourself. You can be fooled. You can get your share of hard knocks. But all this is worth it—the participation, with all of its obstacles and risks, is better than nothing at all, better than maintaining such self-protection that you no longer are active, but become merely a spectator. The meaning here should be clear, especially to you, an Aquarian!

For you, marriage means joy, travel, fulfillment, laughter; your idea of marriage is one that brings forth visions of creative activity, humor and the fulfillment of desires. Sex and love, for you, can and should be an integral part of your life.

Marriage, for you, also equates to friendship; you are more friendly than possessive where a close relationship is involved. You can be an ideal companion. You share both joys and burdens. You tingle with excitement; there is an "electric blue" element which emanates from you, particularly when your emotions are aroused. But they are not easily aroused. You are an experimenter, an analyzer; you want to learn as well as to teach—and this applies to the love and sex areas as well as to others.

Your affections are subject to wanderlust. You are too far-seeing to be limited to just one sphere, or sometimes to just one person. You are sincere in your affections, but you do possess an insatiable curiosity! A sense of adventure is second nature to you and this could create complications. You are, to say the least, a free soul!

Listen: you don't mind breaking rules. But you expect your partner in affairs of the heart to stick to them. As a matter of fact, you can be rigid where morality is concerned—the morality of others, as it affects you. But where your personal activities are concerned, you feel it should be a live-and-let-live atmosphere—as long as you don't hurt anyone. And you cannot imagine yourself hurting anyone. Yes, Aquarius, you are a strange one! Strange in the sense that you like to make and break the rules—but you do expect that others, in relationships with you, should display the utmost loyalty. In a sense, you are much like Leo in this respect—many who study astrology say Aquarius and Leo deserve each other.

You are a generous soul. You are giving. But you are not passionate in the manner of a Scorpio. You are perhaps more intellectual than Cancer, and possibly less so than Libra. You are, like Leo, susceptible to flattery. Since you are not conventional in the first place, a little flattery goes a long way in persuading you to shatter precedent. You are flirtatious, but not in the way Gemini is.

You are really a basic "innocent." When you wander, it is for the sake of satisfying curiosity, not passion. For you, love and sex are subjects which are a part of the human experience, not something separate, mysterious, or to be condemned—or idolized. Like Libra, you seek balance. And like most persons, you need love. But you are more stubborn than most and more likely to insist on your own terms.

Despite the fact that you are an "individual's individual," you do care what others think about your mate or partner. At times you have been guilty of denying yourself happiness because you felt the object of your affection did not live up to the standards *others* might set. You are yourself willing to suffer the slings and arrows, but where someone else is involved, you want acceptance—from *others.*

Free yourself from this syndrome and you will truly be the Uranian individual. And when this occurs, any shackles blocking true happiness will fall away. You will be free. That is the way of Aquarius—freedom! And when this happens, the freedom extends to all areas, including those of sex and love.

How You Relate to the Other Signs

Aquarius is favorably aspected to Sagittarius, Aries, Gemini and Libra. Your sign is not favorably aspected to Taurus, Scorpio or Leo. Aquarius is neutral in relation to Capricorn, Pisces, Cancer and Virgo.

Of course, this represents the briefest view of how you relate to other zodiacal signs. There are further details, nuances, and indications: let's elaborate on some of the highlights.

Aquarius with Aries

Aries affects that part of your Solar horoscope related to short journeys, ideas and activities connected with close relatives. Aries is well aspected to your sign—much harmony is indicated, but little rest!

The Mars of Aries and your Uranus blend to stimulate learning. You can put your ideas to work with the aid of dominant, energetic Aries. The two signs—Aquarius and Aries—may find that they become involved in arguments. The Mars-Uranus combination is volatile. There is life, plenty of it: much action and sudden moves. Aries finds you physically attractive; you are somewhat in awe of Aries. When you relate intimately with Aries, the result can be mental stimulation—or the utmost confusion.

Which it is to be depends, of course, on the complete horoscopes rather than merely Sun sign comparisons. Basically, however, this is not the ideal combination for settling down, for making final decisions. The relationship is fraught with changes, which could involve disagreements among relatives.

It is necessary to decide who is going to be receptive and who is going to be the dominant force in this relationship. Unless this is known subconsciously, or articulated, an otherwise fine association could go by the boards. Uranus and Mars are both symbols of action; if the pull is in opposite directions, the result could be chaos. One or the other—Aquarius or Aries—must be receptive. If this state of affairs exists—one listening, receiving, cooperating—then the relationship between Aquarius and Aries certainly can be expected to flourish.

The signs are harmonious—but for the relationship to succeed, maturity and wisdom must be present.

Aquarius with Taurus

The Venus of Taurus and your Uranus significator combine to encourage originality. Taurus people can aid you in later life. Taurus affects that part of your Solar horoscope related to home, security, property, the authority of a parent. Taurus can infuriate you; you can become disillusioned with current conditions. Taurus causes you to want to break new ground, to shake yourself up; you'll desire more freedom to do things which bring the comforts of home.

On the positive side, this association is invigorating, refreshing, leads to new paths and pioneering efforts. Taurus aids you in accepting and fulfilling responsibility. In any land or real estate dealings, Taurus is beneficial to you. Taurus helps you get your feet on solid ground.

The two signs—Aquarius and Taurus—are not very well-aspected. There are conflicts. Both are strong, determined. But intelligent compromises can be made—and they are necessary.

With Taurus, you search—but perhaps not long enough. There is a tendency to be impatient. But, on a more positive level, you can be determined and patient, you can envision future potential and this will act as an invigorating tonic. The Uranus-Venus combination is a romantic one. But it also depicts emotions subject to sudden rises and falls.

Taurus aids you in putting across business transactions. Your ambitions are fired with Taurus. You'll have confidence in what you want to do, and can obtain financial backing.

In personal relationships, the Taurus-Aquarius team could leave much to be desired. There are changes mood dominate reason. There could be instant attraction, but it might not be long-lived.

The odds for success here cannot be described as better than 60/40. Much, of course, depends on you and the individual Taurus involved.

Aquarius with Gemini

Gemini touches that part of your Solar chart related to children, physical attraction, and creative urges. The Mercury of Gemini and your Uranus significator make this a relationship that can be perfect-or one that does not last. There is little middle ground here. You are stimulated by Gemini and the two signs are favorably aspected. There is everything going for this association, except for a tendency to permit impulse to dominate logic. There are sudden actions and reactions. There are outlandish projects which, however, can be transformed into success.

There is an element of deception here. You tend to idealize the relationship. You skip over the problems and accept the pleasures. This, of course, creates that day of reckoning. The Aquarius-Gemini relationship can be constructive if, at the outset, you are realistic. You can't play games here: emotions run rampant and it's for real. The association could result in marriage and children.

With you and Gemini, there is an aura of illusion. Much that occurs seems to lack a solid base. This could be interpreted as "romantic." Or it could be a kind of fling: a flash that bums bright but lacks real substance.

This is a relationship that has much in its favor. The question is whether you are prepared for it. The attraction is evident, but if you are trying to fool anyone—including yourself—the price in emotional upheaval is dear.

Generally, the Aquarius-Gemini relationship is worth encouraging. The rest is up to you.

Aquarius with Cancer

Cancer affects that part of your chart related to health, pets, work and dependents. The Moon of Cancer and your Uranus significator can combine to make this a good working relationship. With Cancer, you can get a job done. And there will be recognition for what you do. The Moon-Uranus combination almost guarantees publicity.

Cancer helps make you aware of timing, of health, of pacing, of your ability to handle special assignments. You, with Cancer, can get through red tape to accomplish basic tasks.

The two signs—Aquarius and Cancer—go well together when an important job is to be completed. There is much in common, although Aquarius is more willing to make changes. Cancer sticks to patterns, adheres to security.

This is an unusual combination. You could create a product in demand by women. You can break tradition and still come up smelling like a rose. Cancer provides you with a steadying influence: you pursue projects; the pace is even—and there could be a *sudden* recognition of your efforts. Cancer helps call public attention to your completed product, and the Uranus-Moon combination can lead to public acclaim.

Cancer keeps you aware of your basic requirements. Cancer keeps your feet on the ground. This could cause you to rebel, but eventually it proves beneficial. In general, your sign is neutral in relation to Cancer. But if an important task must be completed, Cancer makes you a wonderful ally.

The potential is there: the rest is up to the individual Cancer and to you

Aquarius with Leo

Leo affects that part of your Solar horoscope associated with marriage, public relations, partnerships, how you appear to outsiders. The Uranus of your sign combines with the Leo Sun significator to create an atmosphere of fun and frolic. Uranus and the Sun make a formidable blend; there is much public appeal. Leo would make a wonderful press agent for you. You could also marry a Leo. There is attraction, but a definite explosive quality also exists here.

Aquarius and Leo are signs in opposition. But opposites do tend to attract and fascinate. Both are fixed signs; Leo is of the Fire element and Aquarius belongs to the Air Trinity. The Air-Fire combination can fan a bright flame: it either burns or warms. There doesn't seem much in between where you and Leo are concerned.

For social activity, the combination is excellent. It is also good for travel, writing, publishing. The element of luck seems to persist. Whatever you do with Leo seems to attract public attention, if not notoriety.

There is a definite tendency here for a scattering of forces. Being able to concentrate is difficult. The combination is not meant for detailed work. It is, however, excellent for sales, promotion, a buildup.

For relaxation, for planning a "big event," the Aquarius-Leo team is excellent. As to responsibility for bits and parts, for minor points, for essentials, it could leave much to be desired.

No matter what is said here, you are going to be attracted to a Leo. The experiment could be worthwhile; it certainly will provide its share of excitement. Where the relationship goes from there depends, of course, on the individual Leo and on you, Aquarius.

Aquarius with Virgo

Virgoans are a mystery to you and, thus, have the power to hold and intrigue you—until you solve their riddle.

With a Virgo, you will become concerned with money, long-range security, mystery, the occult, inheritance. You will dig deep to find things out, to erase any clouds of confusion. Your ruling planet, Uranus, combines with the Mercury of Virgo to produce unusual plans, ideas, desires. There is attraction here—the kind of attraction which results from an unknown quantity. You want to know—and Virgo leads you on—either for good or otherwise.

Virgo helps you complete projects. Virgo helps you expand your personal horizons—concern with the unknown is evident. Virgo makes you aware of financial and marital responsibilities. On the positive side, Virgo builds you up and prepares you for the future. On the negative side, Virgo could cause you to become involved in projects which are expensive and not too practical.

With Virgo, you learn lessons, you discipline yourself where ideas and imagination are concerned. Virgo encourages you to explore—there is opportunity for exciting discoveries which can be converted into profit. The key is to be unusual, to seek far and wide for opportunity, and to settle for nothing but the best. On the positive side, that is exactly what Virgo helps you to do.

The Uranus–Mercury combination could make for a good writing or advertising team. A financial advisory service could succeed with Aquarius and Virgo at the helm. Leave the details to Virgo; handle the public relations and promotion yourself. Then the team could come out on top, could have fun—and also show a profit.

Aquarius with Libra

Librans stimulate you mentally—encourage you to travel, to broaden your horizons. The combination of the Aquarius-Uranus and the Libra-Venus spell out creative adventure, satisfaction, fulfillment, attraction. The two signs—Libra and Aquarius—are favorably aspected. Libra touches that part of your Solar horoscope associated with the higher mind, philosophy, publishing and long journeys, including *journeys of the mind.* Libra encourages you to put your knowledge to use.

With Libra you'll be active, your mind won't grind to a halt, you'll investigate, learn, expand, draw on experience. There is a basic attraction here. There are numerous indications of benefit from an association between you and Libra.

Libra helps you form decisions, helps strengthen your convictions, helps make you aware of your conscience, of moral duties. In short, Libra highlights your sense of justice. You are a natural humanitarian, and justice, especially social justice, means much to you. Thus, Libra would mean much to you. Libra gains your respect, sparks your ideals. You feel tenderly toward Libra—you need a Libra, you'll gain from Libra.

On the negative side, Libra could encourage you to over-analyze and procrastinate. On the positive side, Libra urges you to put ideas and *ideals* to work, to write, publish, and advertise.

I would say the relationship would be a good one—I'd encourage it. There can be definite gain. Your wonderful creative sense is awakened by Libra; your sense of the future is crystallized. What was a dream can become a reality with the aid of Libra.

Aquarius with Scorpio

Scorpio affects that part of your Solar chart related to career, basic ambitions, standing in the community, unique honors. The Pluto of Scorpio blends with your Uranus significator to spell a kind of security, comfort and luxury—a unique kind, not the usual domestic variety. Pluto and Uranus represent a sudden and explosive quality.

Aquarius and Scorpio are not favorably aspected, but there is attraction. A mutual goal could unite the two, and, most certainly, a Scorpio can help you attain your goal. This is a most unusual relationship; politics, it is said, makes strange bedfellows. Ambitions, in this instance, can make allies of you and Scorpio. You'll pull together as long as there is a goal. In business, you could succeed with Scorpio. Where there is an objective, the two natives will probably go toward the goal in a straight, true line. Where there is no specific goal, the relationship could be chaotic.

In the personal area, there could be romance. There could be the goal of home, family, domesticity, and acquiring possessions. Both Aquarius and Scorpio have minds of their own, which is, perhaps, another way of saying that you can be stubborn and could meet your match in Scorpio.

Scorpio fires your ambitions. Scorpio encourages you to run for office. Scorpio wants you to go into business for yourself. Scorpio makes you want to accomplish, and elevates your standing in the community. Scorpio builds your image—and could also tear it down. *Don't play games with Scorpio.*

Outline your goals and aspirations. Scorpio is shrewd and finds shortcuts. You make friends, and play a public relations role. Scorpio works behind the scenes and make secret deals. Together, once you understand each other, the two of you could make a formidable combination.

That's the way it is likely to be, Aquarius, when you get together in a serious manner with Scorpio.

Aquarius with Sagittarius

Sagittarius affects that part of your chart related to hopes, wishes, friendships. There is also sexuality involved, an attraction which runs deeper than friendship. Sagittarius and Aquarius are favorably aspected.

The Jupiter of Sagittarius and your Uranus Solar significator combine to stand for excitement, hope, optimism, expansion. With a Sagittarian, you are able to analyze, to appeal, to make yourself popular by giving people what they want and need.

With you and Sagittarius, there is change, travel, variety. Sagittarius enjoys travel and reveres knowledge. Thus, with Sagittarius, you enhance your education. You expand. You leave the precinct and become a citizen of the state, the nation, the world. Sagittarius helps you make your dreams come true. Now, it is not all fun and games. It takes something on your part.

Sagittarius expects you to be bright, versatile, filled with ideas and vitality. Sagittarius keeps you on the move. And as long as you keep Sagittarius fascinated, Sagittarius is on the job, helping you to fulfill your hopes. There is mutual admiration; but there can be chinks in the armor. When these appear, some dreams come tumbling down. The opportunities for happiness are there very much in evidence between Aquarius and Sagittarius. But, with some, opportunities are wasted. It could be that way with you, too.

However, the odds are favorable for Sagittarius with Aquarius. It is up to you. It would be a shame not to take advantage of the chance for happiness which seems to be presented here on a silver platter. The overall verdict is yes for Aquarius with Sagittarius.

Aquarius with Capricorn

Capricorn affects that part of your chart associated with secrets, clandestine affairs, clubs, groups, organizations and institutions. The Saturn of Capricorn and your Uranus significator blend to produce altruistic motives in the two of you. With a Capricorn, you could conduct a successful charity drive, say. Capricorn's Saturn helps steady your Uranus; ideals are transformed to practical action.

There is romance here, too. But it can be the kind of romance that involves forbidden fruit. That is to say, very often your relationship with Capricorn is a secret one. Where the Twelfth House is concerned, there is something under cover, not quite out in the open—and it is your Twelfth House which Capricorn emphasizes.

You are good for Capricorn where money is concerned. In fact, you could pay a Capricorn to provide secrets. Generally, the signs, related, are neutral. There can be a sharing of knowledge. Friction occurs when one feels he is giving more than he is receiving. The relationship could lack a solid base—but Aquarius gets the better of it usually, at least in this astrologer's opinion.

There is something dynamic here; traditions are broken and there is new ground to tread. What was forbidden is revealed. This could be to your benefit, or otherwise. If you have something to hide, it may not be wise to flaunt your relationship with Capricorn.

Your intuition is sharpened with Capricorn. You find out what it is that really is required. This is wonderful for, say, creating a club which appeals to those with unique interests. Capricorn can be a steadying force which aids in getting your ideas off the ground.

That, basically, is the way it is when Aquarius gets together with Capricorn.

Aquarius with Aquarius

An Aquarius, in relationship with another born under the same sign, can be highly successful—if a third person handles the details. With another Aquarius, you tear down and rebuild. You become master builders. You see beyond the immediate. But you tend to overlook essentials. That's why a third person, proficient in handling details, can be an invaluable aid to two Aquarians embarked on a project.

In a personal relationship, there are problems because each Aquarian is so much of an individual-each wants his or her own way. Unless there is excitement and adventure, the relationship could wither.

Aquarius with Pisces

Pisces affects the part of your Solar horoscope that is related to finances and personal possessions. The Neptune of Pisces and your Uranus combine to produce in you two a kind of universal appeal. With Pisces, you can create a product, a service which is in demand and results in profit.

Your sign is of the Air element, while Pisces is of the Water element; you could create waves! One thing is fairly certain: Pisces may well be mysterious, and will hold you in awe. Where you are concerned, Pisces either adds to your possessions, or represents a threat here.

You can be somewhat at a standoff. Both your ruling planets have definite symbolic meanings: you view Pisces in a manner that is reminiscent of two strange beings getting to know each other.

Listen: Pisces will intrigue you and may cost you money. Pisces can also fascinate you and bring in funds. It is that kind of relationship; up and down, favorable, then otherwise. To say the least, it is not going to be even or steady. Uranus and Neptune together do not spell stability. But they do symbolize fascination and challenge.

If you want aid in collecting special objects—say for a hobby—then Pisces can be of help. If you are seeking a bargain, Pisces can he an ally. Pisces is almost psychic, able to ferret out what you might need. But if you are seeking practical, hard-core judgments, Pisces may not be for you. You are a visionary in your own right; Pisces only compounds the asset—or the error, as the case might be.

The two of you—Aquarius and Pisces—have an appeal for the public. You would make a fine sales team—no matter what you're selling. But you don't do particularly well in conventional areas.

That, basically, is the story when Aquarius gets together with Pisces.

Pisces

February 19 - March 20

The Fifth Sector of a chart is related, among other things, to sex. Your Fifth Solar House is Cancer, which gives us some indications about sex and love in relation to you. Cancer is associated with the Moon; your sign, Pisces, is related to Neptune. Your marriage sector is Virgo, signified by Mercury. The planetary symbols which help us in this synthesis are Neptune, the Moon (called a planet for the sake of convenience) and Mercury. For you, love is all engulfing. For you, sex is home and family, a roof over your head; privacy, and enough to eat, satisfaction and emotional stability.

Sex and love, where you are concerned, represent the opposite of sensationalism. Sex is private and you do not boast. Sex, in your scheme of life, is intimate and giving; it is also the receiving of assurance, security. It is romance and imagination; it is not purely physical, as it is with some.

But, listen: you are not always practical about attaining what you desire in this area. Plainly, you can be confused here. You want change and excitement, yet *desire* security. It is no easy task analyzing you in relation to sex and love. You are a romantic to the degree of being, perhaps, impractical. You feel that when you find love, you'll have found all. But you do not go in a straight line toward this objective: your path, instead, is a circle. You often end up where you started: you may travel the high seas in your search, but you light at home, back at the starting point.

Your views concerning sex and love are grandiose: universal appeal, contentment, security—all are tied in a neat, complete package. In actuality, however, you make as many, if not more, mistakes than the average individual. You draw to you people who may take rather than give, who can drain you emotionally *in the name of love.*

Listen: you may not resist temptation enough. Or, if you do, you don't put up much of a fight! You attract to you, very often, the handicapped. This could apply to the physically handicapped as well as those who are emotionally restricted. Your romantic love life represents, at times, continuous trauma. Nothing is simple, it would seem. There are complications. You make resolutions, only to break them. You dream dreams, only to shatter them. You plan, only to reverse your course.

For you, sex is moonlight and roses and violin music; it is beauty and sensitivity. Perhaps your dreams are impossible to fulfill. Yet, I know of many Pisceans who do transform dreams into realities. You can, too. But you may have to apply a greater degree of self-discipline. If you know a person is not only handicapped, but a handicap to you, then you should resist the temptation to be the Great Mother, or Father, the Self-Sacrificer. You can do this without being tough or cruel. Realize, Pisces, you actually will not be much good to anyone if you are no good to yourself. And if you continue to shatter your dreams by accepting unfair burdens, you are hurting yourself and nourishing no one.

Some may claim that you live on emotion. This is true to the extent that emotional excitement, resulting from creative endeavors, tones you up and makes you feel alive. That is different from being merely emotional. You are sensitive to your surroundings, to the moods of people you love. You would think nothing of telling a white lie to spare someone you love emotional bruises. Pisces, you can become involved in bizarre situations associated with love, marriage and sex.

You often create your own code of ethics in this area. You do not feel restricted or bound by man-made rules, by the laws society may dictate. Your heart, your emotions, how you express yourself—when and with whom you consider your private domain. That's why some may find you exasperating. Others see this as part of your charm, your *mystique.* It all, Pisces, depends on who does the looking. As for judging, you seek to judge no person and, in turn, you do not wish to be judged. It is truly your life you are living, you tell yourself.

Nevertheless, you constantly become involved with those who lean, drain, or push responsibility onto your shoulders which shouldn't be there in the first place. You protest, but your actions often belie those statements.

Sex, for you, is of universal importance. You have no doubt about its appeal and you can be a very sensuous individual. You love to eat when you are happy. Food and sex, as is the case with the Cancer-born, often become related. That is, candlelight and fine dining are a part of romance for you; without romance, there is no love.

Unless you have an understanding partner, you can lose what is dear to you. The key is to choose with care. What does this mean? Specifically, it means you need one who is capable of standing on his or her own two feet. What is meant here is that you need an emotionally mature mate or partner. Too often, you draw to you the opposite. You draw people again, who lean or who are dependent. To some extent, this is beneficial because you must feel needed. On the negative side, however, a weak partner will find fault with habits, attitudes. What starts as constructive criticism can deteriorate into petty whining. And this, for you, sounds the death knell to a relationship. Being forewarned here is being forearmed, if you can forgive the cliché.

Listen: your relationships, your marriage and your intimate associations can contain unusual features. There can be a *vagueness* about the legitimacy of an association with you. The partner may not be legally free—or this might apply to *you.* That's why it is necessary for you to choose in the beginning with care so that deception of self—or the other—is avoided.

Ideally, you'll attract someone who is artistic, poetic, has a high degree of appreciation for the arts—someone who is perhaps *mystical,* in the sense that an aura of glamour will persist regardless of the length of the relationship. In fact, the more mysterious your partner, the better the chance for longevity in the relationship.

Above all, don't enter into a relationship for the misguided purpose of uplifting anyone. Marriage does not reform, it merely accents. This applies to both favorable and unfavorable qualities. You should, plainly, not marry in order to reform anyone. The odds are generally against success—and they are particularly against it when you are involved.

Sex, for you, is completion. It is the finishing of a cycle, love given and received. It should be nothing less. You are aware enough to know this—anything less leaves you in a state of expectancy. In some other areas, this is favorable. In the sex and love area, it is not desirable. You require a mature partner—this has nothing to do with chronological age.

Listen: forget your tendency toward self-sacrifice. Start pleasing yourself. You will find, perhaps to your surprise, that this also pleases your heart's desire. You can draw to you emotional cripples. The one sure way of curing that malady is to please by *being pleased.* If you do too much helping, the cripple becomes more crippled. With your acute sense of perception, this should not be difficult to comprehend.

Emotions tend to rule you where love and sex are concerned. You are the opposite of calculating in this area. You are swayed—not only by your own moods, but by those of your partner. Again, maturity is emphasized as a necessity. Without it, you are like a rudderless ship.

The symbolic ruler of your Fifth House, concerned with sex, is the Moon; the Moon is inconstant. There are changes, moods, shades, variations. Combined with your Neptune significator, this can indicate an emotional whirlwind. It is not only *not* always easy for others to plumb your depths, it is sometimes next to impossible for you to know, from one day to the next (depending on your complete horoscope) just how you will react, and what you will react to.

Listen: for you, love should involve all areas of life. Everything you do should be done for love . . . not for money . . . not for "noble" motives . . . but for love.

You are a secretive person, not in the sense that Scorpio is, but in the sense of wanting to leave well enough alone. You don't tell all you know because, in your view (probably a correct one) it would be similar in effect to Samson having his locks sheared: the effect would be to weaken you.

You debilitate yourself when you wear your heart on your sleeve. That is, you open yourself to punishment when your guard is completely down, when you become a dustbin for others. It is, Pisces, only when you combine romanticism with a degree of reality that you make both yourself and your partner happy. Know this and act accordingly. It is a fact that you exude a quiet sexuality. You are the opposite of garish. You are subtle, and you should be linked with one who responds to subtlety. Otherwise, you'll hurt the one you love, to say nothing of the misery you could create for yourself.

You have a tendency to become involved in clandestine situations. For you, intrigue is part of romance.

When love and Pisces get together there is bound to be some intrigue. The key here is not to hurt others, and not, as a result, to hurt yourself.

You are not always what might be termed a practical person. That's true in numerous areas, but is accented in those of love and sex. You don't always choose with an eye to your own benefits. That is the way you are, and if it is not carried to extremes—you can withstand it without hurting. However, if left uncontrolled, this tendency can involve damage. Emotional bruises can swell. Then there's backlash. You might try, as a result of being hurt, to be something you are not. This can become a vicious circle and lead to serious consequences.

Like Gemini, you have a dual nature. You can love more than one person at the same time. Now, much of what I have told you is verified by one of our late, great astrologers. Evangeline Adams said that you often deplete yourself by giving out too much in your desire to help others.

This can be true—and it is applicable in the area under discussion. Too often, you assume responsibility that is not rightly your own. You must, Pisces, permit your partner to carry part of the load. You cannot expect the person you love to be happy if he or she is constantly on the receiving end. Love is obviously a two-way street. You are gentle, often appearing helpless. You are capable of giving tender loving care. But the key is also to receive. When you learn to do this, your life in this area will be more fruitful.

You love nature in that you revere what is natural. To you, nothing is more natural than to love. Again, the key is to receive as well as to give love. Then you are fulfilled and then your dreams do come true.

You have a better sense of humor than some might imagine. You can get yourself involved in intolerable situations and live to laugh about them. Laughing at your own foibles is an invaluable asset. But some"stuffed shirts" don't understand this and may think the laughter is directed at them. Steer clear of those who lack perception.

You can be too indulgent with others. You should raise your standards and make others climb to your level rather than the reverse. Be more confident. Give only when there is a return. Replace noble gestures with give-and-take.

When all is said, you are happier married than single. You are more fulfilled when in love than otherwise—no matter how undeserving your partner may be. No matter what is said here, you will not stop loving even the most outrageous person—if you happen to be in love. But if you do follow some of these hints, you will be opening the door to greater self-satisfaction. And that, Pisces, is an enviable goal—one you can reach if you are determined. Remenber, happiness is a universal goal. You are just as capable of achieving it as the next person.

How You Relate to the Other Signs

You are physically attracted to people born under Cancer; your sign is well-aspected to Cancer, Scorpio, Capricorn and Taurus. Pisces is not favorably aspected to Gemini, Sagittarius or Virgo. Your sign is considered neutral in relation to Aquarius, Aries, Leo and Libra.

You are physically attracted to Cancer and you are drawn to Virgo, but, in the case of the latter, much in the manner that opposites attract each other. With Cancer, there is more of a romantic, carefree attitude; with Virgo or Capricorn, there could be a legal tie, such as marriage, or a legal complication, such as *an inability to marry.* You harmonize physically and sexually with Scorpio, too.

Of course, this represents the briefest outline of how you relate to the other signs of the zodiac. There are further details, nuances, and indications. Let's elaborate on some of the highlights.

Pisces with Aries

With an Aries, that section of your chart associated with money, possessions, and what is valuable, is accented. The Mars of Aries combines with your Neptune to produce either great imagination and idealis—or illusion and deception. When Aries becomes involved in intrigue—it is likely to be with you, Pisces.

You either make money with Aries—or you lose it. There seems to be little neutral ground. Aries, of course, is a Fire Sign—you are of the Water Element. Fire and Water make a difficult combination. Now, Pisces, I tell you this so you can be ready for the challenge—and welcome it. After all, the role of astrology is to forewarn. And, if you are entering a relationship with an Aries, be ready for an individual who is active, enthusiastic and encourages you to invest in your own talents.

There tends to be an element of deception here. Not that you try to fool Aries or that Aries attempts to deceive you, but you two tend to see pictures that do not exist, you tend to conjure up dreams which could be of the pipe-dream variety. What I am counseling, Pisces, is a mature attitude—that both you and Aries face reality. Then you'll recognize a genuine bargain when you come across it.

There is excitement, adventure—and there are problems in this combination. To Aries, you are magnetic, mysterious, secretive. Aries wants to impress you and bring you out of your shell. Aries is likely to succeed, but the proposition might prove expensive for you, Pisces.

You are neighbors of the zodiac, next door to each other. But, nevertheless, there can be a world of difference between Pisces and Aries. Know this and realize you are not likely to reform each other.

Pisces with Taurus

You are of the Water element and quite impressionable. You need some Earth, and Taurus could fulfill that need. Taurus could urge you toward a greater degree of practicality and, at the same time, provide mental stimulation.

Taurus affects that part of your horoscope related to relatives, ideas, short journeys. The two signs are harmonious; a lasting relationship could result. The Venus of Taurus blends with your Neptune to encourage homemaking, a beautifying of surroundings.

With Taurus, you could break from the usual routine. The status quo tends to bore you two, because Taurus stimulates you in a mental sense. You want to break down barriers of restriction. But, simultaneously, you desire security.

You may or may not seek the counsel of relatives in connection with this relationship. But close relatives, such as brothers and sisters, are likely to figure prominently here. You'll either get their approval, or otherwise; not many close to you are apt to be neutral about your association with Taurus.

Many long-lasting marriages have been between natives of these two signs. There is harmony and also a valuable element—the element of humor. Taurus regards you as friendly, pleasant and one who is stimulating. You regard Taurus as one who makes you get up and go.

Some view Taurus as rather plodding, stubborn. But to you, Taurus presents a different picture. You see Taurus' versatile, charming and humorous side.

Specifically, Taurus makes you try and experiment. Taurus encourages you to take notes, to write, to keep in touch with people. Taurus helps you to see the wonders around you and aids you in selecting items that make your personal world a more comfortable—and beautiful—place.

Obviously, this can be a fascinating relationship as well as a lasting one.

Pisces with Gemini

With Gemini, you are made aware of security, long-range projects, home and property. Gemini touches that part of your Solar horoscope associated with the end of a project, and with security in later years. Gemini encourages you to travel, to broaden the scope of your vision, your interests. Gemini tends to make you restless. You two are not likely to be satisfied with the status quo.

Listen, Pisces—Gemini is filled with ideas, and sometimes the ideas are fired at you as if with a machine gun. It is up to you to choose the best, to be discriminating, to be selective. Gemini stimulates your intellectual curiosity. The two signs are not well-aspected; there are problems to overcome. There are obstacles. But, on the positive side, these can be regarded as healthy challenges.

Your Neptune significator, combined with the Mercury of Gemini, indicates an element of confusion—but of the generally happy variety. There is much activity here, but where it ultimately leads is a basic question.

The two signs—Gemini and Pisces—could lack direction when they get together. It will have to be up to you, or to Gemini, to take the lead and see that things follow through to some kind of definite conclusion. Until and unless that occurs, you could be going nowhere. But at least you probably will have fun while doing so.

The relationship could be a time-waster but this depends on the degree of maturity possessed by you and by Gemini.

Pisces with Cancer

You are physically attracted to Cancer. With Cancer, your creative elements can come to the fore. Children could be involved. Also change, travel, variety are indicated. The Moon of Cancer and your Neptune symbolize romance and some intrigue. There is nothing lukewarm about this relationship; it is all the way—or nothing. You will quickly thrive, or equally quickly end the relationship.

Cancer helps you gain greater recognition, broader horizons. The Moon-Neptune blend has far-reaching effects. *Other people are involved.*

You may find that it is not easy to control your emotions when you get involved with a Cancer-born individual. You get started, thinking you can stop at will. But this does not happen always to be the case: one thing leads to another.

On another level, you can complete important projects with Cancer. There is something stable about Cancer which helps to steady you. You seem to find a base of operations; you appear able to know that there is a place to return to, no matter how far you go.

Cancer and Pisces are in trine, which is a favorable aspect. Both are of the Water element. You can be happy with Cancer. But this is no sign to play games with: the results can be serious and permanent—like marriage and children.

Cancer learns from you; Cancer travels with you. Cancer can be elevated through your influence. You, in turn, are vital with Cancer; you come alive. Obviously, there is a great deal of potential for good when Cancer and Pisces combine forces.

Pisces with Leo

Leo relates to that part of your Solar chart associated with work, health, basic issues, pets and special services. The Leo Sun blends with your Neptune significator to indicate practicality in matters that might otherwise be mere daydreams.

The Sun of Leo symbolizes a brightening of your hopes, wishes; Leo can turn Neptunian illusions into working ideas. Leo will keep after you. Leo will remind you of your health, and resolutions with regard to work. Leo will get you going in business.

There is attraction here, because Leo loves glamour and that, Pisces, is one of your basic qualities. Your air of mystery and a chance to reach that pie-in-the-sky. For you, Leo is bright, often enchanting, sexually attractive; but basically, Leo stands, with you, for an opportunity to express practically certain of your unique qualities.

A Leo could drive you to distraction. So much is expected of you in this relationship that there could be emotional turmoil. You might try too hard to impress him or her. Then, of course, your health could suffer. Know this and strive for balance. Leo tends to place you on a pedestal, and might get the mistaken idea that you are tireless. Without meaning to do so, Leo could overwork you or cause you to overexert yourself.

There are positive and negative aspects here. It is an interesting relationship. It could even be fascinating. But the mixture is far from perfect. It needs the seasoning of time to succeed in the long run.

Pisces with Virgo

Virgo affects that part of your chart associated with marriage, partnerships and public reaction for your efforts. The Mercury of Virgo combines with your Neptune Solar significator to mean an increase in your appeal. A Neptune-Mercury relationship spreads, is wide, is big, can be pleasant and funny, but cannot be buried.

Listen: you are attracted to Virgo, but much in the manner that opposites attract each other. You could marry a Virgo. You admire the quickness, the wit of Virgo, even the apparent practicality. Virgo is drawn to your sense of fantasy, of mystery, to your poetic qualities, to your ability to abstract the solid. On the other hand, Virgo can prepare the quick report—and give a quick retort—while you are formulating a theory. Naturally, if a balance between these extremes is achieved, there is a fine blending. There could be a marriage.

On the negative side, this relationship can still be fascinating but nonproductive. Your forces can be scattered; there can be a marked lack of concentration. A kind of dreamlike state can exist. There can be fun and games, but no solid outcome.

One thing: Virgo amuses you. Virgo can make you laugh, even at your own foibles. This, of course, takes us back into the positive area of the relationship. And, on the positive side, your public standing improves. Your image is more palatable. Virgo encourages you to use your imagination for practical purposes, aids you in gaining greater recognition; you become more aware of your potentiality. Virgo, in effect, helps you to become more concrete and less abstract in presenting your views.

Obviously, there is good and bad for you in relation to a Virgo. Much depends on your stage of development—and, of course, on the degree to which Virgo is mature.

Pisces with Libra

Libra accents that part of your Solar horoscope related to other people's money, mystery, the occult. and sex. The

Venus of Libra and your Neptune Solar significator combine to represent an atmosphere of hope through work. With Libra, you can see rainbows; but whether or not you capture them is another story. There is something elusive about your relationship with Libra.

You can be bogged down and restricted here; but, most importantly, you are *aware*. You know what should be done. With Libra, you can face practical issues with *hope*. There is hope for additional financial resources; there is hope that an affair of the heart will have a happy ending. The Venus of Libra and your Neptune signify a romantic combination. It is reality—or the lack of it—that remains the major question; whether the hope is based on realistic thinking, whether there is a real basis for optimism.

Listen: this may all sound complicated. It is. Where the Eighth House is involved, there are complications. Libra is involved with the Eighth House of your Solar horoscope. It is this area of the chart that stands for the occult, meaning what is hidden or largely associated with the unknown.

It is partly because of this that you are attracted to Libra. The benefits of such a relationship are difficult to define. Whatever benefits *do* occur come as the result of work, planning and a piercing of the unknown. Nothing is apt to be handed out on the proverbial silver platter.

Know this and you will have a better chance of success with Libra. Refuse to acknowledge it, and you stack the odds against yourself and Libra.

There is romance here, and there is glamour and mystery. The challenge is to build on a solid base.

Pisces with Scorpio

Your sign is compatible with Scorpio. That sign affects your Ninth Solar sector, having to do with travel, education, philosophy and the ability to perceive what is needed for the future.

The two signs are in trine aspect—favorable to each other. The Pluto of Scorpio combines with your Neptune in a unique manner. It adds up to intuitive knowledge in both of you. You tune in on Scorpio. You learn, and teach: you and a Scorpio might make a wonderful pair in teaching metaphysics. That is, you are a team that could promote the unusual, the unique, the areas which are usually reserved for people with exotic tastes.

Education, places of learning, including special schools; these are emphasized in your relationship with a Scorpio. I stress this because both Scorpio and Pisces are fond of mystery, intrigued by the unknown. Thus, by your setting up a practical program to share these interests, some good could come of it. This would include psychic income, and the earthy variety, too. Personal satisfaction, plus rewards, could result if a Pisces and a Scorpio decide to set up a course, a program, a club, a meeting group devoted to astrology, ESP, or psychic phenomena.

Scorpio finds you physically attractive, and can inspire you. You are idealistic about Scorpio. The two of you could form a mutual admiration society. But the odds are that Scorpio cares for you in quite a direct, earthy manner. You think of Scorpio as someone from whom you can learn, someone who can teach you how to use your talents for a practical, profitable purpose.

What is most important in this relationship, is that there be an agreement to share knowledge. Once Scorpio and Pisces start keeping secrets from each other—the castle of potentiality begins to crumble. Keep your secrets together—but not from each other.

The indications point to a favorable relationship. The rest is up to you!

Pisces with Sagittarius

Sagittarius accents that part of your chart related to career, drive, ambitions, prestige, standing in the community and opportunity for success. The Jupiter of Sagittarius and your Neptune significator symbolize new starts, originality and a degree of selfishness. When together, you'll spread out and then perhaps join in one single line, representing an arrow that shoots directly for the mark.

Generally, the two signs are not considered compatible. But, if determined, this team could build together toward security.

For Pisces, Sagittarius could stimulate a fire, a drive which might otherwise be dormant. For Sagittarius, Pisces represents home and security. But there is conflict. The solution centers on deciding who is going to do the leading, who the following.

With Sagittarius, you will want to elevate your position. You'll want independence. You are more direct in your relationship with Sagittarius than is usually the case. There may be sharp rebukes connected with this relationship. There could be disagreements and battles. But, through it all, there is also likely to be progress.

Listen, Pisces: I would say this is a better relationship on the professional level than it is on a personal one. This means, of course, for starting a business, for promoting a product, for finding room at the top, this combination is favorable. But not so much so for peace, tranquillity, emotional stability. There simply is apt to be too much conflict.

Of course, if you are both mature—and determined—then professional and personal success can be combined. But the odds are against it.

For beginning a project, for an original approach, for creative endeavors for these things—a Sagittarius is good for a Pisces. For emotional contentment, there might be much to be desired.

Pisces with Capricorn

Capricorn affects that part of your chart associated with friends, hopes, wishes, aspirations. The Saturn of Capricorn combines with your Neptune to indicate a harmonious relationship. There is balance here and the signs are favorably aspected. Saturn, representing realism, lends balance to Neptune, standing for the dream. Together, you build—including, possibly, a home and a life together.

On the surface, the signs are very different. Saturn is associated with discipline, and Neptune, with illusion, the freedom to wander, dream, to wax poetic. But, beneath the surface, there are many similarities. Capricorn can be morose. Pisces can brood. Capricorn can drive to the top through sheer determination and a sense of timing. Pisces can wait and wade through a labyrinth to daylight.

Pisces and Capricorn can provide each other with joy. There is physical attraction here. There is also a great chance for domestic harmony. Capricorn views you as an individual of great wit. Capricorn sees you as one associated with short trips. Capricorn is proud to introduce you to his or her relatives. For you, Capricorn represents an opportunity for wish fulfillment. With Capricorn, you can gain—Capricorn makes an especially good financial advisor for you. Capricorn helps your fantasies come closer to something solid, like money or property.

Obviously, then, Capricorn is favorable for you. The relationship, however, takes time to develop, to blossom. Capricorn is apt to be more patient along romantic lines here. Thus, the key is for you to wait, as you're capable of doing, to overcome minor obstacles before plunging in. If you do this, you could be doing yourself a favor.

The vote is *"Yes"* for Pisces with Capricorn.

Pisces with Aquarius

Aquarius affects that part of your Solar horoscope having to do with secrets, restrictions, institutions and clandestine activities. Intrigue often exhibits itself in your relationship with Aquarius. The Uranus of Aquarius and your Neptune blend to stand for the far-reaching. Your goals, with Aquarius, are likely to be humanitarian.

On the positive side, this relationship is good for building organizations that help people. It's especially good for charitable activities. On the negative side, there are undercover dealings indicated that could skirt the law.

When you're with Aquarius, your daring, initiative, and willingness to gamble on your own ideas and abilities are highlighted. Aquarius inspires you to shake off emotional lethargy, to come out of any turtle-like shell. You not only face the world with Aquarius, you determine to do something about it. What you do is either constructive or otherwise, depending on the individual Aquarian involved and, of course, on you.

Basically, with you and Aquarius, there are secrets and you love secrets. There is glamour, mystery—and these are areas particularly suited to your Piscean nature.

Your basic drives, thus, are apt to be stimulated through an association with Aquarius. You have much in common with Aquarius, although this might not be apparent on the surface. Aquarius is attracted to the unknown, to mystery, and is intrigued with time. So are you. But Aquarius is apt to be less patient and more demanding of direct action. A Pisces-Aquarius blend, if properly balanced, could be a formidable one, especially in the areas of television, motion pictures, hospitals and charitable institutions.

Pisces with Pisces

Generally, the relationship between two Pisceans is favorable. Your relationship with another Piscean can produce good results, provided you both possess the determination to give form to thoughts, dreams, ambitions. With another Pisces, there are changes and there could be travel. You become more analytical; two Pisceans can create products that bring joy as well as serve utilitarian purposes.